The *SKIER'S EDGE*

Ron LeMaster

Human Kinetics

Library of Congress Cataloging-in-Publication Data

LeMaster, Ron, 1949-
    The skier's edge / Ron LeMaster.
        p. cm.
    Includes index.
    ISBN 0-88011-982-9
    1. Skis and skiing--Physiological aspects. 2. Kinesiology.
I. Title.
GV854.L45 1999
796.93--DC21

98-30822
CIP

ISBN: 0-88011-982-9

Acquisitions Editor: Martin Barnard
Developmental Editor: Syd Slobodnik
Managing Editor: Katy Patterson
Copyeditor: Jackie Blakley
Proofreader: Sue Fetters
Indexer: L. Pilar Wyman
Graphic Designer: Doug Burnett
Cover Designer: Jack Davis
Photographer (cover): Claus Andersen
Photographer (interior): All photos by Ron LeMaster unless otherwise noted, all photomontaging by Ron LeMaster
Photo Manipulation: Brian McElwain
Illustrator: Jack Hatton; figures 6.2, 6.4, 7.22, 9.7, 9.10, 9.21 and 9.22 by Ron LeMaster
Printer: United Graphics

Human Kinetics books are available at special discounts for bulk purchase. Special editions or book excerpts can also be created to specification. For details, contact the Special Sales Manager at Human Kinetics.

Printed in the United States of America   10   9   8   7   6   5   4   3   2

Human Kinetics
Web site: www.humankinetics.com

United States: Human Kinetics
P.O. Box 5076
Champaign, IL 61825-5076
800-747-4457
e-mail: humank@hkusa.com

Canada: Human Kinetics
475 Devonshire Road, Unit 100
Windsor, ON N8Y 2L5
800-465-7301 (in Canada only)
e-mail: hkcan@mnsi.net

Europe: Human Kinetics
P.O. Box IW14
Leeds LS16 6TR, United Kingdom
+44 (0) 113 278 1708
e-mail: humank@hkeurope.com

Australia: Human Kinetics
57A Price Avenue
Lower Mitcham, South Australia 5062
08 8277 1555
e-mail: liahka@senet.com.au

New Zealand: Human Kinetics
P.O. Box 105-231, Auckland Central
09-309-1890
e-mail: hkp@ihug.co.nz

To my parents, who took me skiing.

Contents

Preface vii

Acknowledgments ix

Chapter 1   Skiing From the Snow Up 1

Chapter 2   The Mechanical Principles of Skiing 5

Chapter 3   The Ski, the Snow, and the Skier's Motion 17

Chapter 4   Turn Anatomy 101 31

Chapter 5   Technique: Controlling Your Interaction With the Snow . . .47

Chapter 6   Fore and Aft 53

Chapter 7   Up and Down 63

Chapter 8   Turning the Skis 87

Chapter 9   Edging the Skis 103

Chapter 10   Lateral Balance 123

Chapter 11   The View From Here 137

Index 139

About the Author 145

Preface

Vic Braden, the noted tennis coach, once told me that every great coach he had known understood the physics of his sport and human movement. That is the subject of this book. This is not a how-to-ski book—it is a book about how skiing works. It is about the fundamental principles and techniques at work in skiing, and how good skiers apply them.

Most avid skiers are, in effect, their own coaches. They improve by watching better skiers, talking with their friends, and picking up tips here and there. Seldom do they work from a knowledge of the sport's basic physical and biomechanical principles. I hope to convey to these skiers a coherent, fundamental understanding of skiing from the snow up; one through which they can evaluate and expand their own skiing.

This book will also be of interest to ski instructors and coaches wishing to expand their knowledge, increase their effectiveness, and pass certification exams.

I expect few of my intended readers to have formal training in physics or kinesiology. None is needed to understand the material. The explanations are based on everyday experience, and no mathematics or arcane notation schemes are used.

In the years I have taught skiers and coached racers, I have found that different people respond best to different types of information. Many do just fine when presented with simple, traditional bits of advice such as, "Start the turn on the ball of your foot" and "Press your shin against the tongue of your boot." Tips like these are effective for most students.

Many skiers, though, learn more quickly and effectively when given information like this: "The ski turns more sharply when pressure is applied to its tip. So to make the ski start turning, it helps to shift pressure forward. Bending the ankle is the best way to do this. You should feel pressure against the tongue of the boot and under the ball of the foot." I could go deeper and explain which elements of the ski's design cause it to turn more sharply in response to increased forward pressure, how bending the ankle moves the skier's center of mass forward in relation to the ski without disturbing any other elements of the skier's body alignment, and how pressing on the tongue of the boot applies leverage to the ski's forebody.

These are examples of what I call *shallow coaching* and *deep coaching*. The first examples, which represent shallow coaching, are directives the teacher makes to elicit a desired behavior from a student. The second example, which represents deep coaching, combines mechanics, technique, and a movement cue to give the student an in-depth understanding of how skiing works, as well as how to ski.

Shallow coaching is appropriate for much of the skiing public. Most skiers who take one or two ski vacations a year learn well with such instruction. They are happy to ski a bit better on each trip while enjoying the guidance and company of a congenial instructor. Skiers who are dedicated to realizing their potential, however, deserve deeper coaching. And regardless of the level of coaching his students require, every professional coach and instructor should have a deep knowledge of skiing.

Understanding the mechanics of good skiing, though, is not enough. Neither is knowing what good skiing looks like. We must know good skiing when we *feel* it, because this is the best information we have to work with when we are actually skiing.

It is a good start to know that shifting pressure toward the tip of the ski when it is edged makes the ski turn more sharply. It is a good addition to know that bending the ankle shifts pressure forward, and turning the femur inward in the pelvis edges the ski. How does the skier know when she is doing these things? By what she feels. The skier should feel that she is twisting the knee inward and pressing the shin against the front of the boot. If the movements are effective, the skier should, as a result, also feel the ski's tip biting into the snow and drawing her into the turn.

To help you make the connection from understanding to practice, then, this book presents movement descriptions of the major technical points discussed. Unfortunately, my subjective experience of a particular force or movement could be different than yours, and you may not always find my description of it compelling. How do you describe the taste of a tomato to someone who has never eaten one? How do you describe the experience of carving a turn to a skier who has always skidded?

This book has two main parts. The first four chapters lay the groundwork for the rest of the book by describing how the skier, skis, and snow interact. Chapters 2 and 3 can be skimmed by readers who do not have a particular interest in mechanics. Chapters 5 through 10 explore ski technique: the movements that you, the skier, perform to make skiing happen.

The book's photographs are of some of the best skiers in the world: racers and mogul skiers from the top ranks of the World Cup circuit, and some of the best instructors in the business. The pictures were chosen for their simplicity, economy, and clarity. In the best cases, they also convey what it feels like to do the right thing. The montages were produced, with a few exceptions, through entirely digital means directly from digital video using an assortment of computer hardware and software.

This book will help you understand the forces of skiing and the movements you, the skier, can make to elicit and control them. It will also teach you to feel them while you are skiing and know when they are right. I hope you find, as I have, that this approach to understanding skiing gives both your knowledge and performance a significant boost.

Acknowledgments

Like all books, this one would never have happened without the help of many people. Martin Barnard and Katy Patterson at Human Kinetics deserve special thanks for putting up with me through the development of this book. Martin, for his enthusiasm for the project and his encouragement when I had my doubts it was worth it, and Katy for her day-by-day attention to and coordination of a thousand details. I would also like to thank Paul Fargis for guiding me through the briar patch of publishing, and Gordon Banks for his advice on matters graphic.

The Vail/Beaver Creek ski school has for the past six years provided me with a forum where I could develop my ideas and shake out some of the bad stuff. The supervisory staff, from Mike Porter, the ski school director, to the supervisors who split classes, assign private lessons, and worry about kids who put their boots on the wrong feet, have supported not only me, but all the trainers and instructors who are committed to dig below the topsoil to find the bedrock of skiing. It is a great ski school, full of great instructors. In particular, I would like to acknowledge Dee Byrne and Steve Holland, who have cut me miles of slack, and who understand that no one knows all the answers, that there are answers no one yet knows, and that everyone's answer deserves to be heard.

I would like to thank Jeanne-Marie Gand and the Rossignol Ski Company for their continued support and express my appreciation to all members of the ski industry who support ski and snowboard competition. Competition is the crucible in which good technique, as well as good equipment, is forged, and it provides us the opportunity to watch and be inspired by the best in the world. Without it, the sport would quickly stagnate.

I want to thank my wife, Dee, and daughter, Alex, for the love and understanding they have shown me year after year; allowing me to immerse myself in skiing to what I'm sure they believe is an unhealthy depth. Every winter they humor my addiction while I teach skiing, clinic instructors, write, and even go free skiing now and then.

Finally, I would like to thank the skiers listed here for providing their time and talent for the pictures in this book. In particular, I want to thank Brian Blackstock, Carol Levine, and Pete Sonntag for demonstrating deliberate errors on request.

Brian Blackstock, 1.1, 4.9, 7.4, 7.17b, 7.17c, 8.7, 8.14.

Dee Byrne, 9.5.

Curt Chase, 11.1.

Christin Cooper, 7.12.

Kelly Davis, 7.7, 9.13.

Chris Dudar, 2.1, 9.23a, 9.23b.

Heidi Israelson, 8.16.

Ron LeMaster, 2.3, 4.2, 6.6, 10.4.

Carol Levine, 3.8, 4.13, 7.9, 7.17a, 9.14, 10.9.

Mike Porter, 2.9.

Pete Sonntag, 2.2, 4.1, 4.10, 4.16, 6.3, 7.11, 9.11b, 10.7, 10.8.

Mickey Stone, 6.8.

Mark Tache, 4.4, 4.14, 8.6, 10.11, 10.14.

Dave Wolfe, 2.1, 2.8, 9.8, 10.1.

Skiing From the Snow Up

None of us skis as well as we'd like. And for most of us, improving is not that easy. We try to recapture those special moments when everything was right and we made turns that infused us with a feeling of perfection. We reflect on the compelling tips we've heard or the visual images of our chosen role models, but our progress is lumpy and elusive.

The most certain path to better skiing is threefold: acquiring a concrete understanding of how skiing works and the components of good technique, a clear image of the world-class skiers performing at their best, and putting a lot of turns under your feet. The words and diagrams in this book will provide you with the first; the pictures, the second. You supply the third.

Skiing is a sport of forces and momentum. When skiing feels good, it is the forces that feel good. We get moving, and then want to be moving in a different direction or at a different speed. Such changes in momentum can only be produced by a force acting on us from outside. The sizable forces that act on us are gravity and the snow's resistance to being compressed and broken up. The snow impresses its forces on us through our skis and poles. We manipulate those tools to get gravity and the force from the snow to shape our momentum into the form we want.

In the next few chapters, we will investigate how the snow and skier interact through the skis, boots, and poles to make skiing happen.

"The Next Revolution"

At least once every decade, some technical ski expert announces that a revolution has occurred in the sport. Either the equipment has changed drastically, or someone (usually the expert himself) has conceived of some new method of skiing that makes most everything you already knew obsolete. Legions of hopeful skiers subscribe to the new technical juggernaut with the hope that they will finally become the skiers they always wished they were.

Hermann Maier.

I make no such claims. It is rare that individuals consciously invent great ski technique. I believe that the development of ski technique is Darwinian: it evolves from the feet of talented skiers all over the world. What works survives. A dominant racer is copied by his competitors. A skier who successfully descends steep, challenging terrain in difficult snow conditions is emulated by her less successful companions.

I also believe that most sound elements of ski technique have been around for decades and decades, and that what has changed over time is the frequency with which those techniques are expressed in the skiing of the sport's best practitioners.

Form and Function

Much of skiing's appeal is stylistic. It would be a dull sport if not for the opportunity it affords us for self-expression. I, personally, have never felt as graceful, fluid, or physically eloquent as I have on skis.

There is, however, a dark side to this attraction. Focusing on form instead of function often prevents skiers from achieving either. People who, for example, want more than anything to ski with their feet close together seldom attain that goal in any but the mildest conditions. Those who pursue the functional path, on the other hand, often learn to ski well enough that they can ski with their feet as close together or far apart as they wish, wherever they are.

I do not mean to imply that you should concern yourself only with technical correctness. Skiing feels great. That is, and should be, the main reason you ski. Keep in mind, though, that the road to good style is paved across the landscape of good technique. See figure 1.1.

From the Snow Up

Years ago I read an article about a successful race car driver that changed the way I thought about skiing. The driver said that everything he did behind the wheel was motivated and judged by the effect on the four patches of contact his tires made with the pavement.

Since then, I have come to think that every element of ski technique should be evaluated in terms of how it affects our interaction with the snow. We turn or slow down because the snow pushes on us and our skis in a particular way, and so we manipulate our skis and align our bodies in a particular way to extract and balance against the force from the snow.

That is my theme. How does the snow push on us to make us turn and slow down? How do our skis interact with the snow to extract those forces? How do we most effectively produce that interaction and then balance against the resulting forces?

Figure 1.1. Physical eloquence, expressed in an airplane turn.

2

The Mechanical Principles of Skiing

Skiing is a sensual sport. We love what we feel when we ski. We even love what we feel when we see another skier make a great turn. And what is it that we feel?

Forces.

The same forces that Sir Isaac Newton definitively characterized with his three elegant laws of motion. The forces that govern the movements of the planets and the balls on a pool table are the same forces that make skis turn, and that make it feel so good.

Forces

In his famous *Lectures on Physics*, the late Nobel laureate and legendary physics professor Richard Feynman said, "Newton's laws . . . say *pay attention to the forces.* If an object is [changing speed or direction], some agency is at work; find it"(volume I, chapter 9, page 3). Skiing is all about changing speed and direction, which is to say, changing momentum. So if we want to understand the mechanics of skiing, to follow Feynman's suggestion, we must search for and understand the forces affecting the skier's momentum.

To start with, we must divide the forces in skiing into two categories: internal and external forces.

Internal forces are those the skier generates with his muscles. They are used to align various body segments, manipulate the skis and poles, and push against the snow to get a desired reaction. Edging the ski by twisting the leg inward is an example of using an internal force to manipulate the ski. Turning the upper body down the hill at the end of a turn is an alignment movement created by internal forces. A quick extension to unweight the skis uses internal forces to push the skier's center of gravity upward.

External forces, on the other hand, are those that act on the skier from outside the body. In the case of a skier, gravity, snow friction, and wind resistance are all

Figure 2.1. Understanding how skiing works requires finding the forces that shape the skier's momentum.

examples of external forces. They are of primary importance, because only external forces can change the skier's motion.

So what is the effect of one of the external forces? Gravity, the primal force of interaction between your body and the earth, gives you momentum. Then, using your skis, you impress your momentum on the snow to evoke from it the forces that make you turn or slow down.

Forces From the Snow

Most everything we do on skis depends on the snow doing something for us. We want to go fast, and the snow obliges by being slippery. We want to slow down, and the snow dutifully pushes on us, resisting our momentum. We want to turn, and the snow pushes us in the direction we want to go.

A skier will only speed up, slow down, or turn if a force from the outside acts upon him. Gravity gives us the speed, and the snow gives us the turning and slowing. We push with our skis against the snow in just the right way, and the snow pushes back.

The snow pushes on a skier in two ways. First, there is friction between the snow and the bottoms of your skis. This is the force that slows you down when you are going in a straight line with the skis pointed straight ahead. Friction can only slow you down: it cannot make you turn. It acts in a direction parallel to the bases of your skis, it is more or less constant, and there is little you can do to change it other than tune and wax your skis.

The other external force from the snow, the one that really makes skiing interesting, is its resistance to being compressed and broken up (figure 2.2). It is this quality of snow that provides the force—pushing on you through the bottoms of your skis—that makes you turn or slow down. It is the force from the snow that propels you through one curving arc and another. It is the force from the snow that addicts you to the sport.

To pack a handful of snow into a snowball takes force and energy. The harder it is packed, the more the snow resists, and the more force is needed to pack it further. You push against it, and it pushes back (figure 2.3). When you push against the snow with your ski, the snow reacts with a force. When you are standing still, the snow is simply reacting to your weight. When you are moving and put the ski at an angle to your motion, the snow reacts to both your weight and momentum. We say that the snow exerts a *reaction force* on the skier.

It is this reaction force that controls your speed and direction. You could say that the rest of this book is about that force: how we massage its magnitude and its direction so that we go where we want to go and do what we want to do on skis.

The snow's reaction force is always perpendicular to the base of the ski, because the base is so slippery. This is a crucial fact that tells us much about how we need to position our skis to get the effect we want.

Sometimes it is easier to think in terms of the *pressure* between your skis and the snow, rather than the force, so you will see that term crop up here and there. Pressure is, simply put, force spread over an area. A person on skis in deep powder

Figure 2.2. The snow's resistance to being packed and broken up controls the skier's motion.

MIKE BROCKWAY

Figure 2.3. Powder snow must be packed until it pushes back hard enough to turn the skier.

applies no less force to the snow than a person of the same weight on foot. But the person on skis puts much less pressure on the snow. He exerts less force on each square inch of snow, and so he does not sink as far as the person on foot. If, on the other hand, a person weighing twice as much comes along on a pair of same-size skis, he will sink in farther because he is putting twice as much pressure on the snow. Controlling pressure and controlling force, then, are the same thing for a skier.

The force from the snow is the accomplished skier's gyroscope. He feels for it, balances against it, and judges the quality of his skiing by it. When skiers learn to feel for and balance against this force, they pass a watershed. They have learned a fundamental lesson of skiing: that how it feels is the most important measure of its quality.

Momentum

Momentum is one of those cosmic fundamental properties of the universe that is a little hard to define. Sir Isaac Newton called it a "quantity of motion"—the product of an object's mass and its velocity. The concept of momentum is more easily understood by observing its effects.

Momentum is that quality of a moving object that makes it hard to slow down or change direction. Put another way, it is that quality your car has when it is moving that wears out your brakes and tires.

Once you are moving on skis, you have momentum. Your momentum will keep you going at the same speed, in the same direction, until some external force pushes on you. That last sentence is very important. You, the skier, will only change direction or speed if an outside force acts on you. This is, essentially, Newton's first law of motion.

The Skier's Center of Gravity

The *center of gravity* is an indispensable concept for understanding the mechanics of skiing. If we were to try to determine the overall effect on a skier of just one force by considering its effect on each of the skier's body segments, we would be faced with a big, difficult job. Instead, we can get the same result much more easily by considering the force's effect on a single point: the skier's center of gravity.

An object's center of gravity is the central point about which all its mass is evenly balanced. If you were to toss the object spinning into the air, it would spin about its center of gravity. An object's center of gravity is almost identical to its center of mass; the difference is so small and subtle that it is insignificant.

For a rigid, symmetrical object like a basketball, the center of gravity lies at the object's geometric center. The center of gravity of an irregularly shaped rigid object, like a boomerang, may lie outside the object itself (see figure 2.4).

Things get a bit more complicated for objects that have movable segments, like the human body. The location of such an object's center of gravity can change as the segments move in relationship to each other.

A person's center of gravity is not a fixed point. For a person standing erect with arms hanging at each side, the center of gravity lies approximately in line with the navel a few centimeters in front of the spine. But the location of the center of gravity changes as the person flexes, extends, twists, and turns. It will often lie outside the person's body. Figure 2.5 shows the approximate location of the center of gravity for a skier in two typical skiing positions.

Each major body segment has its own center of gravity, too, and in some circumstances each must be considered independently. If, for example, the skier relaxes the muscles of the lower back and thighs when skiing into a bump, the centers of gravity of the upper and lower legs, boots, and skis will be displaced upward. Those of the body segments above the hips, though, will actually be displaced downward by gravity. (See figure 2.6.)

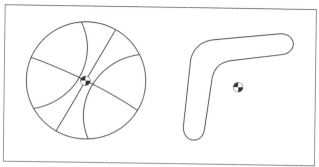

Figure 2.4. An object's center of gravity may lie inside or outside the object.

Figure 2.5. The location of the skier's center of gravity in some typical skiing postures.

Figure 2.6. As Sara Kjellin flexes and extends across the mogul, her upper body's center of gravity travels a different path than that of her lower legs, boots, and skis.

Katja Seizinger and the German Tidal Wave

Katja Seizinger has lead the German women's ski team to a position of international dominance seldom seen in ski racing. Germany has historically fielded teams with occasional singular stars, such as Christian Neureuther, Rosi Mittermier, and Markus Wassmier. Now, the threesome of Seizinger, Martina Ertl, and Hilde Gerg are all exceptional standouts. Never has the ski world seen three skiers of such all-around skiing talent and skill all competing on the same team at the same time.

This is how the three Germans fared up in the 1998 World Cup standings:

- Overall: Seizinger 1st, Ertl 2nd, Gerg 3rd
- Downhill: Seizinger 1st, Ertl 21st, Gerg 5th
- Super-G: Seizinger 1st, Ertl 4th, Gerg 7th
- Giant Slalom: Seizinger 6th, Ertl 1st, Gerg 9th
- Slalom: Seizinger 12th, Ertl 5th, Gerg 3rd
- Combined: Seizinger 2nd, Ertl 3rd, Gerg 1st

Their results at the 1998 Nagano Olympics were equally impressive. Of the fifteen medals awarded for women's alpine events, six of them—more than a third of the total—went to these three women: three gold, one silver and two bronze. Their loot included a clean sweep of the medals in the combined event.

Of the three, Seizinger is the greatest "touch" skier paying the least attention to being a technical perfectionist. Her hands may not always be in just the right place, but her skis are. She has a loose and gentle feel for the snow that has helped make her a constant threat in downhill and super-G since the early 1990s, and without question, the speed-event woman of the decade. She is also the only woman in history to win consecutive Olympic gold medals in the same alpine event (downhill), and one of only two women to win three Olympic alpine gold medals.

Gerg, whose style is simple and solid, is the preeminent slalom skier of the three, although she also excels in speed events, as evidenced by her

SPORTS FILE / DENNIS CURRAN

1997 World Cup title in super-G. With no flourishes or extraneous movements, Gerg simply seems to put her outside ski on the line she wants to ski, and stands on it. Among other accomplishments, she won the gold medal in slalom at the 1998 Olympics.

Ertl is the best giant slalom skier and the most complete technician. Her movements are consistently precise and fluid, her balance is dead-on, and her line judgement is impeccable. Rarely will you see Ertl be forced to make a big on-course adjustment or recovery. Interestingly, Ertl has the least gender-specific style of the three, and in this regard she resembles her biggest rival in giant slalom, Deborah Compagnoni.

This powerful trio spans the spectrum of key skiing skills and talents, and so provides a complete textbook on modern ski racing.

Working With Forces, Momentum, and the Skier's Center of Gravity

Forces and momentum all have two salient attributes: magnitude and direction. Gravity, for example, acts toward the center of earth. When you sit down on a chair lift, the chair exerts a force on you in a direction opposite that of gravity, and just a bit greater in magnitude, and therefore lifts you away from the center of the earth.

Throughout this book, I will use arrows, the standard graphical device used by engineers, to represent forces and momentum. An arrow's length and direction will correspond to the relative magnitude and direction of the force or momentum it represents.

The force of gravity acting on something can be represented by an arrow pointing toward the center of the earth. A skier's momentum can be shown by an arrow pointing in the direction the skier is traveling, its length proportional to the skier's speed and weight. The exact lengths of the arrows we use are not important, just so long as the relative lengths of the arrows used in the same picture reflect the relative magnitudes of the things they represent.

Slowing and Turning Are Changes in Momentum

Slowing down corresponds to a decrease in the magnitude of the skier's momentum. This will happen only if the skier meets with a force acting at least partially in opposition to her direction of travel.

The skier turns when her momentum changes direction, and this will happen only if a force pushes on the skier from the side. Figure 2.7 shows how these effects can be isolated or can happen at the same time, depending on the direction in which an external force acts on the skier.

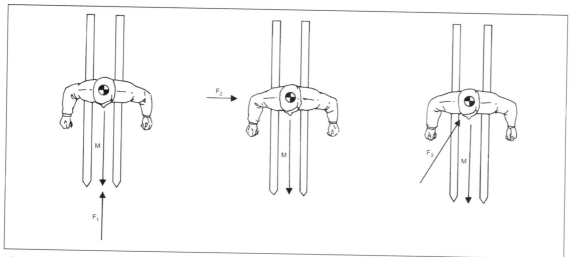

Figure 2.7. The force F_1 reduces the skier's momentum M because F_1 directly opposes it. F_2, because it acts perpendicular to M, changes the direction of the skier's momentum, but not its magnitude. F_3 both slows and turns the skier because it acts both from the front and the side.

Combining Forces

When two or more forces act on a body, they have an additive effect, as if the body were acted on by a single force. Put another way, we could replace those forces with a single force, and the body would react in exactly the same way. That single force is called the *resultant* of the other forces.

When making a turn, you experience both gravity and centrifugal force. (We will not quibble here about the nature of centrifugal force, which some argue is not a true force. For our purposes, it is quite acceptable to consider it one.) As shown in figure 2.8, these two forces have a combined effect that determines how far you must incline into the turn to be in balance, as well as the magnitude and direction of the snow's reaction force.

It is easy to find the resultant of two forces. We simply draw an arrow for each force, with their tails anchored to the center of mass, then draw a box (strictly speaking, a parallelogram) using those arrows as sides, as shown in figure 2.8. A new arrow marking the diagonal of the box is our resultant.

If we need to, we could add a third force now by combining it in the same manner with the resultant of the first two. Any number of forces could be added together in this way. Throughout this book we will be considering how various resultant forces on the skier, the ski, and the snow are formed, and how they must be managed.

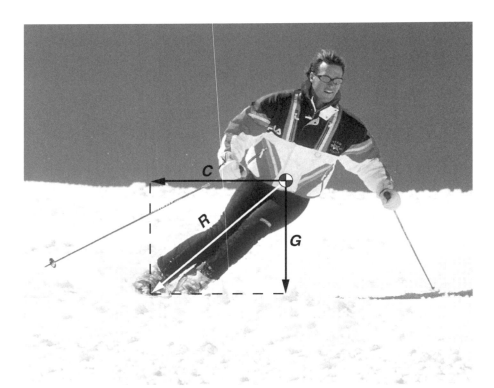

Figure 2.8. Centrifugal force, C, combines with the force of gravity, G, to form the resultant force, R, acting on the skier.

Resolving a Force Into Components

Besides combining forces to find a resultant, we will also at times want to break down a single force into components.

   To resolve a force into components, we draw a box with that force as its diagonal. The sides of the box attached to the force's tip or tail are then two components that could make up that force. In figure 2.9, we see the force the snow exerts on the ski and skier resolved into two components: one that acts to slow the skier (S_d) and another that makes his path bend (S_t).

   Notice that we could draw any number of different boxes for which the original force serves as a diagonal, and indeed any number of component pairs could be drawn for that original force. The pair we choose is determined by what we want to find out. In the case of figure 2.7, we are interested in how much of the force from the snow is making the skier turn, and how much is slowing him down.

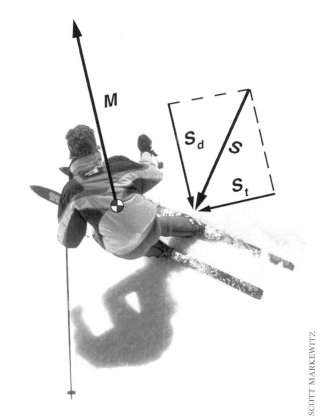

Figure 2.9. The reaction force from the snow, S, can be broken into two components: S_d, which slows him down, and S_t, which makes the skier turn. Their angles to the skier's momentum, M, not his ski, determine their effect on his motion.

Twisting Actions

The forces and momentum we have talked about so far all act in straight lines. They are linear. There is another class of force and momentum related to twisting actions.

Torques

A *torque* (pronounced *tork*) is a twisting force. You crank a corkscrew into a wine bottle by applying a torque to it. When you turn a bolt with a wrench, the force you apply to the handle puts a torque on the bolt. The handle acts as a lever arm on the bolt. The longer the handle, the longer the lever arm through which the force works, and the greater the torque.

Angular Momentum

The type of momentum we have been discussing so far is, to be precise, *linear momentum,* and is related to the body's velocity and mass. A body that is spinning has *angular momentum.* A top spinning in one place has no linear momentum, but plenty of angular momentum (see figure 2.10).

Figure 2.10.   Three full back flips and three full twists. Serious angular momentum in World Cup aerial competition. All the skier's angular momentum is acquired before he leaves the take-off.

Angular momentum is related to how fast the body is spinning and what we might call its *swing weight,* although *moment of inertia* is the proper technical term. A body's moment of inertia is related to how its mass is distributed and the axis about which it is spinning. A ski has a much smaller moment of inertia about its longitudinal axis (the axis about which it rotates when you edge it) than it does about a vertical axis (the one about which it rotates when you pivot it into a turn). And a short, fat ski will have a smaller swing weight than a long, skinny ski of the same weight. So, because its smaller swing weight requires less torque to create angular momentum, short skis are easier to swing into a turn than long ones. And although a ski pole's weight may be constant, its swing weight is different, depending on which end you hold.

The greater an object's swing weight, or moment of inertia, the more torque is required to give it a certain amount of angular momentum. That is why short skis are easier to pivot into a turn than long ones. It is also why a ski pole is tapered: that shape puts the pole's center of gravity closer to the handle than the tip, thereby reducing its swing weight.

Equilibrium, Toppling, and Compensating

A body is stable as long as the resultant of all forces acting on its center of mass passes through the body's base of support. If that resultant passes outside the base of support, the body will start to topple. This may sound like a bad thing for a skier, but in fact it is necessary and desirable for making parallel turns. As we will see in chapter 10, the ability to topple and recover in a deliberate and controlled way is the essential skill that separates would-be expert parallel skiers from the real experts.

Consider the box in figure 2.11. As long as the force acting on it (in this case, gravity) acts through its base of support, the box is stable. As soon as that force falls outside the box's base, the box topples, because the reaction force from the ramp cannot line up with and oppose gravity. The wider the box's base, the farther it could tilt before toppling. A smaller base would make its balance more precarious.

A skier in a wide stance is like a three-legged stool: he has a stable base of support and, barring sharp unforeseen jolts, is stable as he moves along. If he were to stop moving, nothing in his stance would need to change to prevent him from falling over. An expert in a narrow stance is more like a broomstick balanced on your outstretched hand. He usually has all his weight balanced over the single, outside ski, and is seldom in perfect, static balance. Rather, the expert is constantly making small adjustments in response to changes in force from the snow, just as you must adjust your hand to keep the broomstick from falling over.

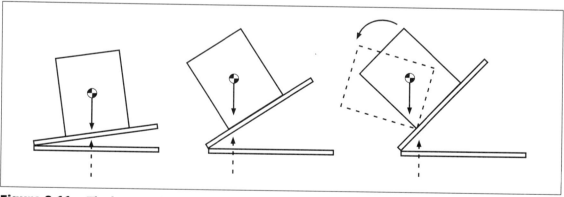

Figure 2.11.   The box topples when its center of gravity moves beyond its base of support.

3

The Ski, the Snow, and the Skier's Motion

Our skis are the instruments we use to extract and manage the force from the snow. Through their clever manipulation, we get the snow to push on us with just the right strength and in just the right direction to control our motion.

In general, I will present things from the point of view of the skier, rather than that of a stationary observer. Rather than talk about the uphill ski or downhill ski, I will talk about the *inside* or *outside* ski (that is, the ski that is to the inside or outside of the turn). Also, I will frequently talk about one thing or another being in relation to the skier's direction of travel, which is also the direction of the skier's momentum.

In almost all skiing, it is the outside ski that makes you turn. In fact, it is generally desirable to ski with all your weight on one foot at a time. But even when skiers split their weight between their feet, the large majority of it goes to the outside ski. So when I talk about "the ski," I mean the outside ski, unless I explicitly state otherwise.

Alberto Tomba.

Getting a Grip

What makes a ski slip? What makes it hold? From their first day on the snow, all skiers grapple with these questions.

When we say we want the ski to hold, we really mean that we want the snow to exert enough force on us to prevent any sideways movement. We often settle for less. Whether we hold or not seems black and white. Slipping, on the other hand, comes in shades of gray. We can slip a little, but still extract enough force from the snow to get where we want to go. Or we can slip a lot and hope we don't end up in the parking lot.

Our intuition tells us that the more we edge the ski, the better it will hold; that a more radically edged ski is like a sharper knife. This is only half-true. The physical mechanics that determine whether a ski holds or slips are not complicated, but neither are they obvious.

Penetrating the Snow

If the ski is to extract any force from the snow, it must give the snow something to push against. If the snow is soft, the ski will penetrate it easily. The snow will then give way under the ski until it is compacted sufficiently to resist further packing.

When the snow is hard, there are two keys to making the ski penetrate the surface and hold. The first is to apply all the force available to as small an area as possible, maximizing the pressure on the snow. This is the primary advantage a sharp edge has over a dull one. A dull edge spreads the available force over a larger area than a sharp edge. Its shape also gives the snow a microscopic ramp to push on that will encourage the ski to slip.

Figure 3.1. The force that 1998 Olympic slalom champion Hans-Petter Buraas applies to his outside ski, R, can be resolved into two components: one that makes it penetrate the snow, R_p, and another that makes it slip, R_s.

Applying all the force to one ski is the other key to making the ski penetrate hard snow. The force you apply to the ski's edge has two components, as shown in figure 3.1. One acts parallel to the snow surface, and tries to make the ski slip. The other acts perpendicular to the snow, trying to drive the edge down into it. To make the ski hold on hard snow, you must maximize the second of these components. When you put weight on both your feet, the geometry of the situation causes more slipping force to be applied to the outside foot than the inside one. At the same time, it also puts proportionately more penetrating force on the inside ski. You are squandering, so to speak, some of your available penetrating force on a ski that does not have much slipping force applied to it. As you move pressure from the inside ski to the outside ski, the penetrating force on the outside ski increases faster than the slipping force. You maximize the ratio of penetrating force to slipping force, and you apply the most pressure to the edge, when all your weight is on one ski.

The Critical Edge Angle

The second condition required for the ski to hold is that the surface against which the snow is pushing, the base of the ski, must be held at the best angle for the snow to push effectively on it.

Most skiers share a common misconception: that the angle between the edge of the ski and the snow surface determines how well the ski holds. This is not the case. Rather, it is the angle between the bottom of the ski and the force applied to it by the skier that determine this.

Ask yourself this: Why is it hard to put your ski on when it is on a slope? It is hard because the ski is slippery, and the snow can only push on it perpendicular to its base (figure 3.2). This force is not lined up exactly opposite to gravity, which is the other force acting on the ski. The unbalanced component of gravity pushes the ski sideways toward the bottom of the hill.

What do you do to make it easier to put your ski on? You jam the ski into the snow to make a level step on which it can rest while you finagle your boot into the binding. The level step helps because now when the snow pushes perpendicular to the bottoms of your skis, it is pushing in the exact opposite direction of gravity, and thus completely opposes it. The key is that the surface against which your skis are pushing is perpendicular to the force acting on it—gravity.

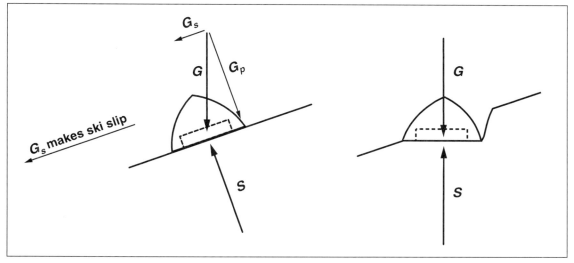

Figure 3.2. What makes a ski slip, and what makes it hold? Both skis in this figure, which are placed sideways on a slope, are acted on only by gravity, G, and a reaction force from the snow, S. Because the ski is slippery, S can only act perpendicularly to the skis' bases. For the ski on the left, S can only oppose G_p, the component of G that is also perpendicular to the ski's base. This leaves an unbalanced component of gravity, G_s, that makes the ski slip. The ski on the right feels no unbalanced forces, and does not slip.

When you finally get your ski on, you are faced with the same proposition: make sure the bottoms of your skis cut a step in the snow that is perpendicular to the force applied to the ski (gravity), or you will slip.

Things change a bit, but not much, when you are in a turn. Now you are subject to the combined effect of gravity and centrifugal force. The resultant of these two forces is no longer directed toward the center of the earth, but inclined toward the center of the turn. To keep from slipping, the ski needs to be supported by a step that is perpendicular to this combined force. In both situations, the traverse and the turn, it is not the angle of the ski's edge to the snow that determines whether the ski slips or holds, but the angle of the ski's edge to the resultant force applied to it. I call this the *critical edge angle*.

Consider the two skis depicted in figure 3.3. R is the force the skier applies to the ski, S is the reaction force from the snow, and e is the critical edge angle (the angle between the bottom of the ski's edge and the force applied to it by the skier). The base of the left ski in figure 3.3 is perpendicular to R. It cuts a small step in the snow surface, and the snow responds with a reaction force exactly equal and opposite to the force applied to it by the skier. The ski holds.

The base of the right ski in figure 3.3 is not perpendicular to the force R acting on it. That is to say, its critical edge angle is less than 90 degrees. It cuts a step in the snow that slopes away to the left from the force R, and so the ski will slip.

Turning and Slowing

Just about everyone has, at some point, stuck a hand out the window of a moving car and flown it up and down through the wind. When the hand is flat, with the palm parallel to the pavement, it stays in one place. Given a little twist, it climbs or dives. Turned so the palm faces straight ahead, it neither climbs nor dives, but meets the maximum resistance from the wind trying to slow its forward motion. See figure 3.4.

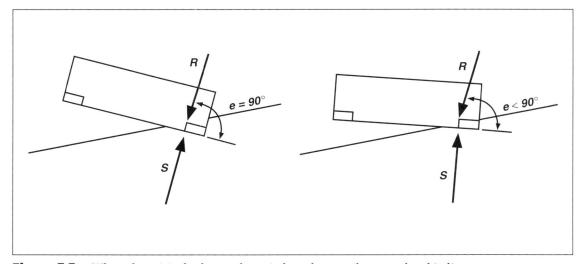

Figure 3.3.   When the critical edge angle, e, is less than 90 degrees, the ski slips.

Your hand exerts a force on the air as it moves forward through it, and the air answers with a reaction force. The air resists being compressed, and so it pushes back.

Regardless of how you hold your hand, the air is always exerting a force on it toward the rear of the car, trying to slow it. When the hand is at an angle to the wind (an aeronautical engineer would call this its *angle of attack*), there is another component of force: one that pushes the hand up or down. The backward force on the hand is smallest when the hand is perfectly level, and greatest when the hand is turned perpendicular to the wind. In neither of these positions is there any force pushing the hand up or down. Between these two extremes, though, the air's reaction force has a vertical component.

The graph in figure 3.5 shows, in approximate terms, how the upward component of the air's reaction force grows progressively as the angle of attack goes from 0 degrees up to around 50 degrees. As the angle increases from that point, the upward force decreases. It finally dwindles to nothing when the angle of attack is 90 degrees. On the other hand (no pun intended), the component of the air's reaction force pushing the hand back continues to grows steadily as the angle goes from 0 to 90 degrees.

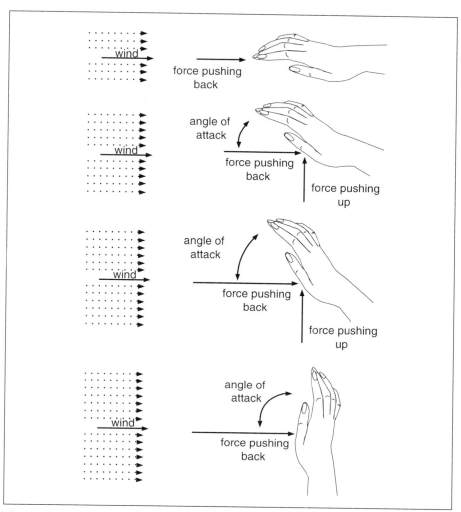

Figure 3.4. Forces on a "flying hand".

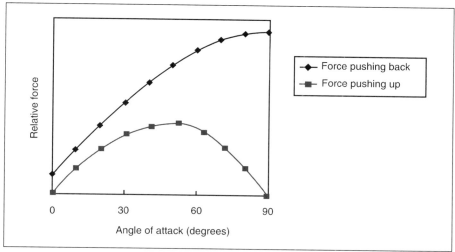

Figure 3.5. How the forces on the flying hand change with the angle of attack.

The Steering Angle

The snow's reaction force pushes on the ski (and the skier) in much the same way as the air on your flying hand. What we called the hand's angle of attack, we call, in the case of the ski, the *steering angle.* A ski running straight is like the hand with its palm parallel to the road. No force acts to change the ski's direction of travel. Put at 90 degrees to the skier's momentum, the ski elicits a reaction force from the snow that acts only to slow the skier. With the ski at any angle in between, the snow pushes on the skier like the wind on an angled hand. Some of the force acts to slow the skier, and some of it acts to change her path. By varying the ski's steering angle, the skier varies the proportion of slowing and turning components of the snow's reaction force.

A small steering angle results in a broad turn. A larger steering angle, up to a point, produces a sharper turn. Beyond that point, increases in the steering angle cause more slowing, but less turning.

Many skiers do all their skiing at steering angles of 60 degrees or more. Their skis work not so much to change their direction of travel as to keep their speed down by sliding sideways. They achieve their goal of speed control, but at the expense of one of skiing's great pleasures: the feeling of carving a round, clean, efficient turn, which generally requires smaller steering angles.

Don't get me wrong. Expert skiers throw their skis sideways in many situations, such as making turns on very steep slopes, and slowing down in confined spaces. But they separate the intention of slowing down from that of changing direction; an important distinction.

Before you can turn, your ski must turn. It all comes down to steering angles. The flying hand moves up and down when it is at an angle to the air through which it is passing. Your direction of travel changes when the middle of your ski is at an angle to it.

Look closely at the bottoms of your skis. I'll bet that the biggest dings are right under the middle of the ski. The tip and tail will look much better. Get your skis waxed and look at the bases after a half-day of skiing. The wax will be worn off under the foot, but not under the tip and tail.

This is direct evidence that the big forces in skiing happen directly under your feet. These are the forces that make you, the skier, turn. The middle of the ski does the work of changing your direction of travel, largely due to its steering angle there, as shown in figure 3.6a. The tip and tail are simply not stiff enough to push very hard on you, and therefore don't have enough force to make you turn.

Compared to the force a skier applies to a ski, that is to say his weight and centrifugal force, the ski is not very stiff. It typically takes only 10 to 15 pounds to flatten a ski on the snow. From this point on, as you add more weight and centrifugal force, the pressure builds under the middle of the ski, but not much elsewhere.

What this tells us is that the tip and tail of the ski do little to make the skier turn. What do they do, then? They make the ski itself turn.

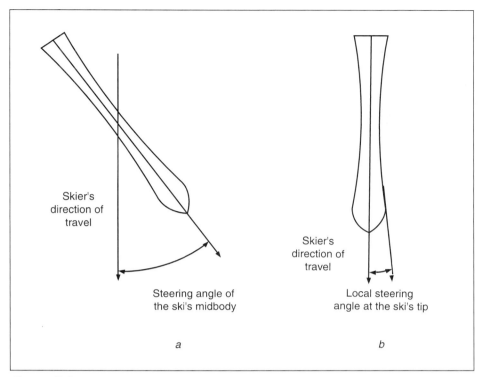

Skier's
direction of
travel

Steering angle of
the ski's midbody

a

Skier's
direction of
travel

Local steering
angle at the ski's tip

b

Figure 3.6. Because of its shape, the ski's steering angle varies along its length.

How the Ski Turns Itself

Skis are subtle tools, with a spectrum of design points that make them do certain things very well. The particular features in which we are interested right now are *side-cut, longitudinal flex*, and *torsional flex.* These features work together to make the ski, if it is edged, turn as it moves forward. I call this the ski's *self-steering effect.* All skiers use it to control their turns, both carved and skidded. The sidecut and flexing characteristics of modern skis accentuate the effect. When you see a skier make smooth, round turns with no noticeable pivoting of the skis, you are watching a skier manipulate the ski's self-steering effect.

Sidecut

Skis have an hourglass shape, called *sidecut.* Its interesting effect is that the ski's steering angle varies continuously along its entire length. It is greatest at the tip, and decreases steadily toward the tail (figure 3.6b). Because the tip always has a greater steering angle than the rest of the ski, the ski will turn as it moves forward. The ski turns itself.

Figure 3.7 shows a ski with a simplified and exaggerated sidecut. It has a bow-tie shape, with the waist directly under the skier's center of gravity. Assuming the ski is edged, the snow exerts a greater force against the edge of the forebody than the tail, because the forebody's steering angle is greater.

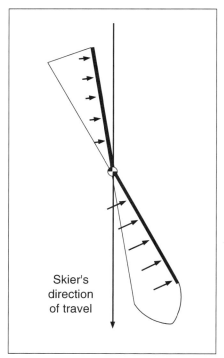

Skier's direction of travel

Figure 3.7. The deflecting force the snow exerts on the ski varies with the angle between the edge and the skier's momentum: the steering angle.

The forebody and tail each act like separate flying hands. They both draw reaction forces from the snow that push the ski in the same general direction, but the forces on the forebody are greater. As a result, the ski pivots around its center as it moves forward.

Torsional Flex

If you grab a garden hose in both hands and twist, the hose is flexing in torsion. This type of flexing is a key characteristic of each ski. In coordination with the ski's side-cut, it determines how aggressively the ski's tip and tail bite when the ski is edged. The stiffer a ski is in torsion, the greater will be its self-steering characteristics, all other things being equal. On the other hand, a ski with a deep sidecut that is also very stiff in torsion will be edgy and difficult to pivot or make slip.

Longitudinal Flex and Reverse Camber

Longitudinal flex is the name for the ski's tip-to-tail stiffness. When the ski flexes this way, it bends like a bow into what is called *reverse camber* (figure 3.8). This accentuates the effect of the sidecut, increasing the relative difference between the tip and tail's steering angles. The more deeply the ski is bent into reverse camber, the greater the tip's relative steering angle, the smaller the tail's, and the greater the ski's self-steering effect. The depth of the ski's reverse camber is determined by how much force the skier applies to the ski and how well the tip and tail bite, which the skier can control by edging or flattening the ski.

Figure 3.8. This skier's outside ski is bent into reverse camber, making it turn as it moves forward.

Taking advantage of the ski's sidecut and longitudinal flex, the skier can make a gradual turn by simply rocking the ski on its edge. If the tip of the ski points in the direction the skier is going, the edge of the ski's forebody has a small steering angle, as shown in figure 3.6b. As the edge engages the snow, this local steering angle brings a reaction force from the snow against the tip that makes it turn slightly as it moves forward. This in turn creates a small local steering angle in the ski's midbody, which brings a reaction force that changes the skier's direction of travel.

While the critical edge angle dictates how well the ski holds, the angle between the edge of the ski and the snow bears strongly on how sharply the ski will turn.

Hermann Maier

© TIM HANCOCK

Herman Maier's first season on the World Cup, 1996–97, was promising: he won a super-G event. This win did not, however, provide any foreshadow of what was to come in just his second season on the tour: he won, in overwhelming fashion, the men's World Cup overall championship, the super-G and giant slalom World Cup titles, and Olympic gold medals in super-G and giant slalom. He was the first Austrian to win the overall men's World Cup since Karl Schranz took the very first crystal globe in 1972.

What many people see when they watch Maier race is a hell-bent daredevil who is willing to take any risk to win—a daredevil who sometimes loses in spectacular fashion, as he did in the 1998 Olympic downhill in Nagano, Japan. There he took what is surely the most memorable Olympic crash since Jim Barrow's fall in the 1968 Grenoble Olympic downhill.

A closer look at Maier, however, reveals a skier of incredible technical sophistication and depth, whose technical abilities allow him to take a riskier, more direct line than his rivals—and get away with it. He seldom crashed in the 1997–98 season, but he made many spectacular recoveries.

In his aggressive, no-holds-barred style, Hermann Maier is reminiscent of Primin Zurbriggen, the great all-around Swiss skier of the 1980s. His exemplary technique, on the other hand, speaks of his upbringing in Flachau, Austria, where he began teaching skiing at the age of 16 in his parents' ski school. His years as an instructor have undoubtedly helped provide the foundation of exemplary technique on which Maier relies.

All of the technical giants of the sport, Erikson, Sailer, Killy, Thoeni, Stenmark, Tomba, Zurbriggen, and Girardelli, have dominated giant slalom at some time during their careers. It is noteworthy that Maier has made one of his biggest marks in that discipline, unseating Michael Von Gruenigen, who had been virtually unbeatable the previous season, as World Cup champion. Like Zurbriggen, whom he most closely resembles, Maier is also the man to beat in super-G and he is a consistent contender in downhill.

Maier has clearly raised the bar in the world of men's alpine ski racing, and the rest of the field is now playing catch-up.

When the ski is tipped on its edge, the ski's sidecut gives the ski more bite at the tip and tail. This increases the pressure at the ski's extremities and the depth of the reverse camber into which the ski is bent. The greater the angle between the ski's edge and the snow, the deeper the reverse camber and the greater the ski's self-steering effect.

Why Skis Have Curved Sidecuts

Skis are not shaped like the one in figure 3.7, of course; their sides are curved. It is enticing to think that this curve corresponds to the curve the ski will follow on the snow, but this is an oversimplification. Skis have curved sidecuts so the skier can control the ski's self-steering effect by edging and flattening the ski. The precise curve of a ski's sidecut is carefully designed to coordinate with its longitudinal and torsional flex characteristics to produce a ski that behaves smoothly and predictably as it is edged and flattened, and the distribution of pressure on the ski is shifted forward and backward.

No ski is perfectly rigid in torsion. They all twist when loaded and edged. Because of this flex, the ski grips most in the middle and less and less aggressively toward its extremities. The critical edge angle of the ski in figure 3.9a is 90 degrees under the skier's foot. The middle of the ski will hold well. But because the ski flexes in torsion, the tip and tail will have poor grip, therefore will not be able to make the ski turn. In figure 3.9b, the ski has been edged more so the critical edge angle at the tip is 90 degrees. Now the tip and tail will hold well, increasing the ski's self-steering effect and making the ski turn more sharply.

Pivoting the ski changes the steering angle of every point on the ski by the same amount. Edging and bending the ski, on the other hand, increases the steering angle of the forebody more than the tail. By moving the distribution of pressure forward on the ski, the skier creates deeper bend in the forebody, accentuating the self-steering effect. By shifting it toward the tail, the skier reduces the load on the ski's forebody, reducing its bend and the effect.

All other things being equal, a ski with a deeper sidecut will exhibit more self-steering effect, as will a ski stiffer in torsion, because either will give the ski more bite at the tip and tail. These design points, along with others, are carefully balanced by the ski engineer to produce a ski with good skiing characteristics. None can be viewed in isolation from the other to determine how any given ski will behave.

Figure 3.9. Because the ski flexes in torsion, its critical edge angle varies along its length. As the skier edges it more, the ski bites better further toward the tip and tail, increasing its self-steering effect.

The Boot Is Part of the Ski

Once the boot is in the binding, it is effectively part of the ski. Think of it not as a shoe on some sort of alien steroids, but as your ski's handle: a handle you control with your leg and foot, rather than your hand.

The part of the boot that gives you the most control over the ski is the part that wraps around your lower leg: the cuff. To control the edge of the ski, you push with your leg against the side of the boot. Pushing against the boot's front or back puts pressure on the ski's tip or tail.

As we have seen, a ski turns more sharply when it is edged and pressure on it is shifted forward. So to encourage the ski to start a turn, it helps to edge the ski and shift pressure toward its tip. To do this, you should push against the inside front corner of the outside ski's boot (figure 3.10). To stop the ski from turning, push against the back of the ski (figure 3.11).

Figure 3.10. 1998 World Cup slalom champion Ylva Nowen presses her right shin into the inside front corner of her boot cuff to make the ski bite and turn.

Figure 3.11. Siegfried Vogelreiter uses the back of his boot to shift pressure to the tail of his outside ski to complete a giant slalom turn on a steep hill.

Controlling the Ski's Self-Steering Effect

A good, versatile ski has a lot of different turns built into it. If you only stand smack dab in the middle, however, you will not see too many of them. By judicious adjustment of the ski's critical edge angle and the fore-aft distribution of force along its length, you can make it tighten or broaden its turn. Sometimes the ski will carve as it turns, and sometimes all or part of the ski will slip.

You have six basic options.

* Edging the ski more will make it turn sharper, because doing so engages the ski farther toward the tip and tail, where the edge has a greater local steering angle. Flattening the ski will make it turn less.

* If the ski is very flat or in light contact with the snow, you can twist the ski using techniques we will investigate in chapter 8.

* If the ski is not edged very much, shifting pressure to the tail will make it slip more than the tip. This approach is used by many skiers whose main objective is to ski with their feet locked together. We see them straight-legged, leaning back, and wiggling around in an effort to shove their tails to and fro. This technique is fraught with problematic side effects.

* If the ski is edged and weighted, shifting pressure toward the tail makes it go straighter. Moving pressure back takes both bend and bite out of the forebody, letting the stiffer, straighter middle portion of the ski have more effect on the ski's track.

* Moving forward on an edged ski makes it turn more sharply. The shift makes the tip bend more, describing a tighter arc on the snow. It also makes the tip bite into the snow harder, so that it has a greater effect on what the ski does.

* Aggressive forward pressure coupled with an insufficient critical edge angle will make the tip bite and the tail slip, especially at the end of the turn. Too much forward pressure is the main reason a ski's tail will slip downhill at the end of the turn. Skiers often refer to this as the tail washing out. It is also the cause of the downhill stem at the turn's end that many skiers find themselves unable to shake, even after years of lessons and attentive skiing (see figure 3.12).

Often the skier's natural response to this last problem is to try to edge the ski more. Most skiers do this by twisting the knee inward and forward. While this does increase the critical edge angle, it also increases pressure on the tip, making the tail slip even more.

The solution to this problem is to back off from the tip of the ski a bit. Straightening the ankle, as explained in chapter 6, will take pressure off the tip and enable the whole ski to grip.

SCOTT MARKEWITZ

Figure 3.12. Too much pressure on the ski's forebody makes the tail slip, especially at the end of the turn. This is often interpreted as a downhill stem. The solution is to increase the critical edge angle and/or shift pressure back a bit.

Turn Anatomy 101

All turns are not created equal. All share a common structure, but those components can look quite different from one turn to the next. In this chapter, we examine the various species of turns and their similarities and differences, and introduce some terminology we will need later.

The Phases of the Turn

Different things happen in different parts of every turn, and to give us a framework for their dissection, we need to adapt a clear vocabulary for those parts. We will talk about turns in terms of their phases: initiation, control, and completion, as in figure 4.1.

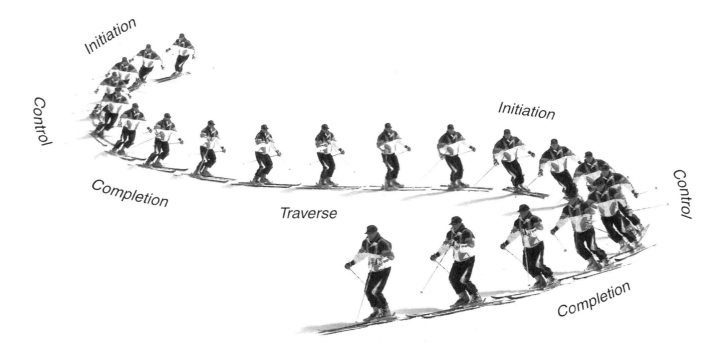

Figure 4.1. The phases of two basic turns.

When turns are linked directly to one another, with no intervening traverse, the completion of the first flows seamlessly into the initiation of the next, and together form a transition phase, as shown in figure 4.2.

Initiation

In the initiation, you establish the ski's initial steering angle needed for the turn. You do this so the snow, acting through the ski, will make your path bend during the next phase of the turn. In the initiation phase, you also align various body segments among themselves and with your skis so that you can balance properly against the forces of the turn that will arise in the control phase.

Three things happen in the initiation:

1. Your body inclines toward the inside of the turn, relative to your outside ski, in anticipation of the centrifugal force you will encounter in the upcoming control phase. In other words, your center of mass moves closer to the center of the new turn than your outside foot. Accomplishing this accurately and dynamically distinguishes skiers of different abilities more than anything else.

2. Your skis change edges. Strictly speaking, only one edge has to change. Whichever edge or edges were supporting the skier before the entry into the new turn, a different edge or edges will now do the work of making the turn happen.

3. At least one of your skis must establish a steering angle relative to your momentum. This could be as small as the angle provided by the ski's sidecut, as in figure 4.3, or a pivot of more than 40 degrees, as in figure 4.4.

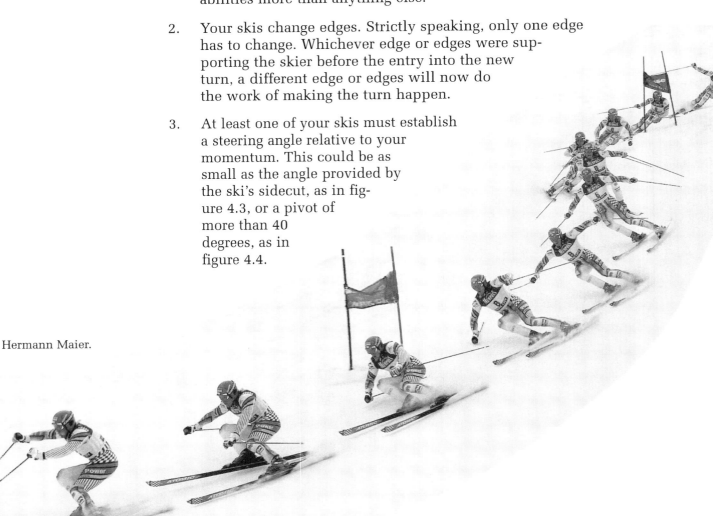

Hermann Maier.

Control

The control phase is where the snow makes you turn (figure 4.5). Significant lateral force between the ski and the snow makes your path bend, and the ski, due to its self-steering effect, turns itself as it moves forward.

To take advantage of the ski's self-steering effect, you will control the distribution of pressure fore and aft on the ski as well as the ski's critical edge angle to get the shape of turn you want. You will also use other means to control the ski's steering angle. In short turns, especially on a steep slope, the control phase may be very short, or nonexistent.

Completion

In the completion phase, you want to stop turning and either go into a traverse or start a turn in the other direction. To do this, you must eliminate

Figure 4.2. The transition starts with the completion phase of one turn and ends in the initiation phase of the next. Once started, the transition cannot be stopped until the skis engage the snow in the new turn.

the lateral force from the snow that was making you turn. You do this by reducing the ski's steering angle and your inclination into the turn. These two actions must happen together in a coordinated fashion. Reducing your inclination reduces the ski's edge angle, which reduces its self-steering effect. Reducing the self-steering effect reduces the ski's steering angle, which in turn reduces the lateral force from the snow, requiring less inclination to remain balanced.

Figure 4.3. At 70 mph, Hannes Trinkl initiates a big turn simply by rolling his outside ski onto its edge and letting its shape go to work.

In some turns, simply reducing the ski's edge angle will allow it to straighten out, putting the skier into a traverse. In many dynamic, large-radius turns, the skier will also encourage the ski to stop turning by shifting the distribution of pressure toward the tail, as Deborah Compagnoni does in figure 4.6.

Transition

Until they attain a certain level of proficiency, skiers make turns that have distinct initiations and completions, separated by traverses. Advanced skiing starts when the traverse between a skier's parallel turns disappears. The completion of one turn and the initiation of the next merge seamlessly into a transition phase (see figure 4.7).

Figure 4.4. On a steep, moguled slope with cut-up powder, this skier pivots his skis more than 40 degrees to initiate his turn.

Figure 4.5. Canadian Thomas Grandi skis through the control phase of a giant slalom turn.

Now, instead of picturing a turn as going from traverse to traverse, we can view it as going from fall line to fall line. For an expert skier, the transition is a continuous succession of movements that, once begun, cannot be stopped. The timing and coordination of these movements is crucial.

The transition begins when your body is released from the forces of the turn, and its momentum carries it in a straighter line than your feet are traveling. This is where the expert feels release and the illusion of acceleration. In the extreme, the skis pop, the feet fly to the outside of the new turn, and the body shoots down the hill in anticipation of the force that will develop when the skis engage the snow to make the next arc.

There is a particularly crucial moment in the transition. It is the point at which your center of gravity's path crosses over the path of your feet. The skis at this moment are running straight and flat on the snow. This makes them easy to pivot. Consequently, the more accurately the skier can sense the crossover point, the more easily he can turn his skis without unweighting to disengage them from the snow. For the same reason, it is the point at which the pole plant can have the greatest turning effect on the skier.

Figure 4.6. Deborah Compagnoni of Italy completes a giant slalom turn by moving pressure from the forebody of her outside ski to the tail. This makes the ski turn less and eventually run straight, releasing her from the turn.

Figure 4.7. 1998 World Cup overall champion Katja Seizinger executes a seamless transition from one turn to the next.

Deborah Compagnoni

Deborah Compagnoni often says she pushes herself to only 90 or 95 percent to win a race. This is not bragging. As a young racer, Compagnoni was a risk-taker. She describes herself as having had a "dangerous style" in her early years of skiing. This caught up with her when she reached the World Cup circuit and suffered three serious knee injuries over a four-year period. Since then, she has traded abandon for technique, physical power, and dead-accurate line judgment. She now takes only those on-course risks she needs to win, and no more. And she wins frequently, often by big margins.

It is Compagnoni's incredible line judgment that, perhaps more than anything else, separates her from her competition, especially in giant slalom. In the event that most richly rewards good on-the-fly line selection, she rarely has to make in-course corrections. While it is common to see a first-seed giant slalom racer tighten or loosen the radius of a turn in mid-arc to compensate for a slight misjudgment earlier in the turn, such adjustments are rare for Compagnoni.

Like fellow Italian Alberto Tomba, she is a simple, compact skier. Her arms are even quieter than Tomba's, and her balance is unshakable. Also like Tomba, she trains by herself, apart from the rest of the Italian women's team. This is not an expression of arrogance, simply a recognition of what works best for her.

Deborah Compagnoni constantly seeks innovation, both in her skiing and in her equipment. She was among the first World Cup racers to adopt the new generation of super-sidecut skis that appeared in the mid-1990s. When Dynastar, her supplier, first made such racing skis for giant slalom, they only produced them in one length, intended for male competitors. Still, because Compagnoni saw the inherent advantage of the new design, she raced, and repeatedly won on them. Pushing the envelope again in 1998, she was disqualified from a slalom in which she posted the fastest time for competing on a pair of skis

© TIM HANCOCK

that was narrower than the minimum required width at its waist.

Physiologically, Deborah Compagnoni is toward the narrow-hipped end of the spectrum of women ski racers and she skis with a bit less hip angulation and counter than many of her competitors. In many ways her stance is similar to that of Martina Ertl's, winner of the 1998 World Cup giant slalom title and Compagnoni's biggest competitor in giant slalom.

The consummate big-race competitor, Compagnoni is the only alpine skier to have won gold medals in three winter Olympics. She has, in addition, won three World Championship gold medals and an Olympic silver. And since she seems to have put her earlier daredevil, injury-prone style behind her, we might see her continue to compete, and win, at the highest level of international competition for many years to come.

The Virtual Bump

Because you make turns on a slope, a surface at an angle to gravity, the total force between you and the snow varies throughout every turn. Even on a perfectly smooth hill, the effect of making turns is just like that of skiing through bumps. The better the skis hold and the tighter the turn, the greater the effect.

In a sharply carved turn made on a smooth slope, for instance, the skier will feel light at the top of the turn and heavy at the bottom. This is because the gradient that the skis are on changes through the course of the turn in the same way it does when you ski off one bump and into another.

On the left of figure 4.8, we see the track of two idealized turns. The right of that figure shows the gradient on which the skis are running at each instant in those turns. At the beginning, the skis are across the fall line, on a relatively flat grade. As the skier approaches the fall line, the grade becomes steeper and steeper, as if the skier were passing over a bump into a dip. When the skier turns out of the fall line, the skis come onto a flatter and flatter grade. The gradient traced by the skis, as shown on the right, looks just like the profile traced by a skier running through bumps.

Another way to look at the same phenomenon is shown in figure 4.9. The component of gravity that is not opposed by the snow always points down the fall line. At the start of the turn, centrifugal force points in the opposite direction, making you feel a bit light. At the end of the turn, the two forces are pointing in the same direction, making you feel heavy. In between, the total force you feel builds continuously. This, again, is just like skiing first into the trough between two bumps, and into another bump at the end of the turn.

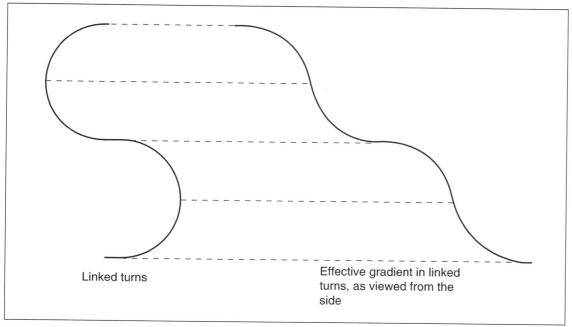

Linked turns

Effective gradient in linked turns, as viewed from the side

Figure 4.8. As a skier moves through turns on a smooth slope, the effective gradient changes as if he were skiing through bumps.

Gravity ———▷
Centrifugal force ———▷
Resultant ———▶

Figure 4.9. Gravity and centrifugal force interact through the course of the turn to make the skier feel lighter at the start, and heavier at the end: the same as if he were skiing in bumps.

This effect, which I call the *virtual bump*, plays a fundamental role in all of advanced skiing. It is the effect of the virtual bump that makes it easier to start a turn from the end of the previous turn, rather than from a traverse. It is one of the tools an experienced skier uses to make skiing less work when she is tired or just wants to relax and cruise. For the world-class racer, the effect reaches magnitudes that make it a formidable, disrupting influence. How to exploit and control the virtual bump is addressed in chapter 7. See figure 4.10.

A Taxonomy of Turns

I am going to start with a gross over-simplification and say that there are three types of turns: skidded turns, carved turns, and checked turns. In truth, these are idealizations that seldom, if ever, occur in their pure forms. Still, most turns are dominated by the characteristics of one or another of those basic types.

Figure 4.10. Crossing the virtual bump. Even though the hill is smooth, the dynamics of the turn have the same effect on the skier as a mogul. Despite this skier's flexing through the first three frames, he is projected upward slightly by the virtual bump.

✳ In a skidded turn, the ski slips sideways as it moves forward. Flying out the window of a car, your hand makes skidded turns.

✳ In an ideal carved turn, the ski never moves sideways while it is engaged with the snow. This is the sort of turn bicycles make.

✳ In a checked turn, the skis stop moving momentarily at the turn's completion, then are pulled into the next turn by the skier's momentum. If you visualize how a slinky toy marches down a flight of stairs, you can grasp how checked turns work.

High-performance skis are designed with curved shapes and flexural characteristics that help them execute the ideal carved turn. It is convenient to think these characteristics define the well-carved turns that a specific pair of skis will make. The side-cuts of most skis are circular arcs, and the relative size of the radius of a particular ski's sidecut does provide a rough indication of how tightly the ski likes to turn. But as we saw in chapter 3, other design points, especially the ski's torsional and longitudinal stiffness, play a significant role in the size of turns the ski will carve. So as we consider carved, skidded, and checked turns, keep in mind that there is little black or white about any of the turns we make.

Carved Turns

Imagine you are holding a large glass mixing bowl, and that lying in the bottom of the bowl is a large steel ball—the kind you see in a pinball machine. Now, imagine picking up the bowl and moving it in a swirling motion, setting the ball in a circular orbit inside the bowl.

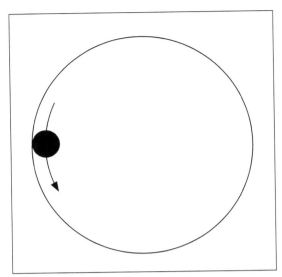

Figure 4.11. A ball circling in a bowl provides a good model for a carved turn.

You have just created a carved turn simulator (see figure 4.11). The mechanics that make the ball move in a curved path are much the same as those you employ to make a turn on skis.

The ball has inertia and momentum, which would make it go in a straight line if it were not for the bowl. The shape of the bowl defines the shape of the path in which the ball moves. More precisely, the ball's path is defined by the reaction force the bowl exerts on it, pushing it toward the center of the bowl. (What we commonly call centrifugal force is what the ball "feels" in response to the bowl pushing on it.)

Because the bowl is curved, at every instant the ball is rolling into a surface that is at a slight angle to its path. In skiing terms, this is the bowl's steering angle at each instant, and is what makes the bowl push the ball out of its naturally straight path.

In a pure carved turn, the ski cuts a groove in the snow, which it then slides along much like the ball rolls along the side of the bowl. At every moment, the groove has an infinitesimal steering angle under the skier's foot, and so the turn is extremely efficient. How sharply the groove curves dictates how sharply the skier turns.

Two key features, then, define carving:

*   The ski turns itself as it moves forward. As long as the ski engages the snow, the skier does not twist or pivot it.

*   The ski moves only forward, and not sideways.

For this to happen, the ski's self-steering effect is used to cut a curved groove in the snow. The groove must be strong enough to support the force exerted on it by the ski, and the ski must not jump out of the groove. Carved turns are the sort of turns racers aspire to because they dissipate a minimum amount of the skier's momentum. See figure 4.12. Experts aspire for these too, because in many situations, carved turns give the best control, are the most secure, and feel good, too.

Pure carving is an ideal seldom, if ever, realized. Most turns made by most skiers involve a fair amount of skidding. Even the turns that feel carved to an expert skier have some degree of skidding in them.

Skidded Turns

A ski making a skidded turn moves sideways as it moves forward. This is the basic difference between the skidded turn and a carved turn. Otherwise, the fundamental mechanics that produce both types of turns are the same. The middle of the ski engages the snow at a steering angle to the skier's momentum, and the snow pushes back on the skier to turn or slow her. In both cases, the force that the snow exerts on the skier has a turning component. In the case of an ideal, perfectly carved turn, there is no slowing component. There are no perfectly carved turns, however, and as soon as a turn deviates from the ideal, some slowing component appears. All the turns we make in the real world have some slowing component, and the distinction between what we call carved and skidded turns is not absolute.

The more a turn is skidded, the less efficient it is. The less smooth it is, too, because the ski does not absorb irregularities and shocks nearly as well when it hits them sideways as when it encounters them with its tip. See figure 4.13 for an illustration of skidded turns.

Figure 4.12. Kristina Koznick of the United States carves a slalom turn. Koznick placed second in the 1998 World Cup slalom standings, and was by far the tour's most consistent performer in slalom, finishing all nine races in sixth place or better.

Figure 4.13. Skidded turns. The skis are at a large steering angle throughout the entire control phase. Compare these steering angles with those of Kristina Koznick in the previous figure.

Figure 4.14. Checked turns.

Checked Turns

These are the sort of short-radius turns an expert makes on a steep hill when speed control is critical (figure 4.14). He finishes the turn with an edge set, making the skis stick in the snow at a large steering angle. In the extreme, this feels like hopping down a flight of stairs.

With the edge set, the skis almost stop. Then, to the extent that the thigh, buttocks, and lower back muscles contract, the motion of the skier's center of gravity will slow, too. If the skier intends to make another turn, he will let his momentum carry him across his skis, toward the center of the next turn, pulling the skis with him.

The Initial Steering Angle

I've said it before, and I'll say it again: before the skier can turn, the ski must turn. It must have a steering angle, however small.

Any particular ski is capable of carving arcs of a particular radius, but no smaller. How big is the "bowl" that a modern ski carves in the snow? This is hard to quantify. Simply looking at the radius of its sidecut will not tell you. When a ski is tipped up on edge and pushed into reverse camber, the radius gets smaller. At the same time, the ski will flex in torsion, twisting such that the tip and tail flatten to a lesser edge angle than the middle of the ski, and somewhat reducing the ski's self-steering effect. In sum, a modern ski with a deep sidecut might describe on the snow an arc with a radius as small as 30 feet. This is a big arc. Think of a circle, 60 feet across. That is the smallest arc the edge of our archetypal ski will slice. As long as the turns you want to make are no smaller than the radius your ski can carve, you can start them by simply rocking the ski on its edge and letting it pull you into the turn.

This is the sort of turn depicted in figure 4.15a. The bowls that correspond to the ski's natural carving radius match up perfectly, and the ball never encounters a steering angle larger than the infinitesimally small steering angle of the bowl's curve. This curve provides the initial steering angle for each turn the ball makes.

Figure 4.15b illustrates turns in which the ball must change direction more quickly than the natural curve the bowls alone will produce. Each time the ball leaves one bowl, it encounters the side of the next at an angle sharper than the natural steering angle of the bowl's side.

This second scenario provides an idealized description of how a skier can make a carved turn smaller than the natural turning radius of the ski. The skier starts by pivoting the ski to an *initial steering angle* from which the ski is made to carve an arc of its natural radius. This is, in fact, how the vast majority of carved turns are made, both by recreational skiers and World Cup racers.

Note that the angle between the ski and the fall line is not the issue here. It is the angle between the ski and your direction of travel, your momentum, that counts. If you are traveling in a shallow traverse, the ski can have a significant steering angle well before it reaches the fall line, and so can generate a useful turning force. If, on the other hand, you are making short turns that do not stray far from the fall line, not much will happen until the ski is well through the fall line.

How you go about establishing that initial steering angle is a key element of every learning progression. When you ski in a wedge, each ski always has a steering angle (figure 4.16). All you need to do to initiate a turn is to make one ski dominant, either by putting a majority of your weight on it, or twisting it to a larger steering angle than the other ski.

As skiers get better, they learn ways, some of them subtle, to guide both skis parallel to an initial steering angle. Their purpose is always the same: to get the midbody of the ski to a steering angle that will extract the lateral force from the snow that will turn you in the direction you want to go.

Figure 4.15a. When the radius and spacing of turns are just right, they can be linked and carved without pivoting the skis.

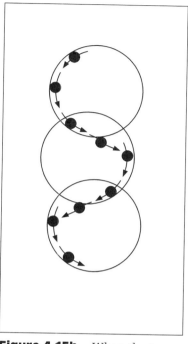

Figure 4.15b. When the turns get shorter, the ski will not carve perfect arcs from turn to turn, but must be pivoted to an initial steering angle, from which it can carve to the turn's completion.

The Size of the Angle

How big an initial steering angle do you need for a particular turn? That depends on the turn. The sharper the turn, the greater the initial steering angle. Small initial steering angles provide a progressive buildup of

Figure 4.16. In a wedge, the skis are always at a steering angle, one in either direction.

reaction force from the snow and a smooth entry into the turn, but are inappropriate for short turns, especially on steep terrain. A large initial steering angle makes for a dramatic buildup of reaction force. Recall, too, that when the size of the steering angle gets beyond a certain point, you get more speed control and less direction change.

Turns in which the ski follows its edge from start to finish, that is, turns with very small initial steering angles, are fine on broad, groomed runs that do not demand you turn in any particular place. More and more of our skiing terrain seems to be going in that direction, too. But when you seek more challenging terrain, you will need greater initial steering angles.

Large initial steering angles are needed for short turns on steep slopes. At one end of the spectrum is the sort of turn made by extreme skiers in very steep couloirs, where the skis are pivoted nearly 180 degrees before they engage the snow. Careful study of World Cup racers also shows significant initial steering angles in many slalom and giant slalom turns, as Kjetil Andre Aamodt illustrates in figure 4.17.

Line Selection for Carved Turns

World Cup racers make many slalom and giant slalom turns with sizable initial steering angles. When the turns are not sharp, little initial steering angle may be seen. But when the turns get tough, initial steering angles of over 40 degrees are not uncommon (figure 4.18). So, how do you know what the initial steering angle should be for any given turn?

The way a skier judges the steering angle is similar to how an archer aims an arrow. An archer aiming at a target does not point the arrow directly at the bull's eye. Knowing that the arrow will follow a curved path from the bow to the target, she aligns the arrow with that curve at the point where it meets the bow (see figure 4.19).

Figure 4.17. Kjetil Andre Aamodt initiates a turn on a gentle section of the second run in the 1997 Park City World Cup giant slalom. Aamodt begins with a slight uphill stem, and by the time his outside ski engages the snow in the fifth frame, it is at a steering angle of around 30 degrees. After having posted only the 28th fastest first-run time in this race, Aamodt switched to a more deeply-shaped ski and raced into 2nd place overall, winning the second heat with this exceptionally fast run.

Figure 4.18. Christian Mayer starts a giant slalom turn on a steep pitch with a large initial steering angle. The skis do not engage the snow until the final frame, having been redirected a good 40 degrees.

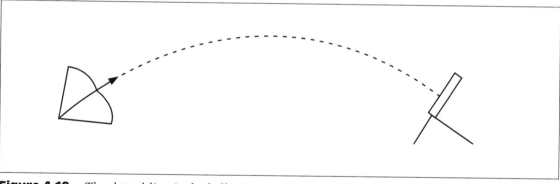

Figure 4.19. The dotted line is the ballistic curve the archer knows the arrow must follow if it is to hit the bull's eye. To aim accurately, the archer lines the arrow up with that curve.

The skier's problem is similar to the archer's, and the world-class racer has developed his own version of its solution. Before starting a turn, the racer knows where he wants it to end, and in what direction he wants to be going at that point (figure 4.20). Knowing from experience how sharp an arc he can carve, the racer in effect sees that arc on the snow, beginning at the turn's intended exit point, and progressing back up the hill (figure 4.21). The skier then initiates the turn by pivoting the ski until it is aligned with that arc at the point it intersects his current path. When the ski lines up with the arc, the racer engages it with the snow and carves to the turn's completion, as figure 4.22 shows. The angle between the arc and the skier's direction of travel coming out of the previous turn is the initial steering angle for the turn.

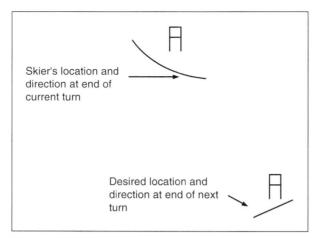

Figure 4.20. A carved turn starts with the skier identifying the turn's intended exit point and the direction the skier wants to be going when he gets there.

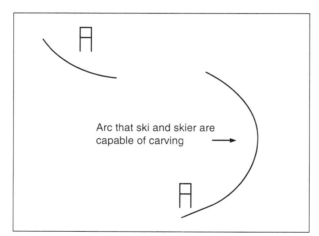

Figure 4.21. The skier visualizes the curve that the skis can carve to the turn's exit point.

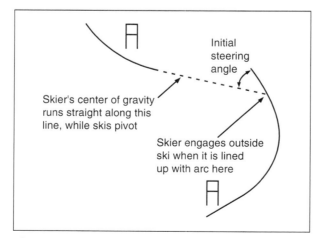

Figure 4.22. The skier pivots the outside ski to align it with the arc that it will carve to the turn's exit point.

Becoming deft with a ski or an arrow requires learning the shapes of the curves they make. In archery, the curves vary with the pull of the bow, the distance to the target, the wind, and so on. In skiing, too, many factors contribute: the shape, stiffness, and condition of the skis; the size of the turn; the skier's speed; the slope of the hill; the character of the snow; and more.

Many skiers start their turns with excessive steering angles. They fling their skis sideways into the turn, resulting in a barely controlled power slide. By oversteering the ski from the start, they never give it a chance to slice, but instead make it scrape.

Unfortunately, most of these skiers never develop an appreciation for fitting their skis to a round, smooth arc. Skiers who insist on always skiing on challenging terrain (steeps and moguls) are especially prone to learning only to pivot and skid. They need to understand that making many turns of all sizes at all speeds on smooth, moderate terrain is essential to the development of well-rounded ski technique. I often seek out smooth, gentle runs and practice making slow, clean, carved turns. It is a great exercise in balance, control, and snow sensitivity.

Controlled skidding and slipping are required in many turns to achieve a desired line and speed. Still, the extent to which the skidding can be reduced generally makes the turn smoother, more controlled, and more enjoyable. And it is fair to say that skidding comes far more naturally to skiers, so that carving skills are the ones requiring deliberate tutelage and practice.

Technique: Controlling Your Interaction With the Snow

So far, we have talked about how the snow interacts with the ski and the skier to control the skier's speed and direction. These are matters of fact. The remainder of this book addresses ski technique: the movements that you, the skier, make with your body to initiate and manage these interactions. These are sometimes matters of opinion.

There are many ways to turn a pair of skis, some better than others. Like most people who have spent much time thinking about it, I have my own opinions, and I will warn you that much of the rest of this book is based on them. And before inflicting them on you, I should tell you how I've arrived at them.

My approach has always been to study the best skiers in the world, distill the common elements of their skiing styles, and analyze what I get. This statement begs a question: Who are the world's best skiers? I believe that the best skiers are those who are judged as the best by the most objective criteria. This means World Cup racers, World Cup mogul skiers, and free skiers who ski the most challenging terrain on the planet and survive. I reject as role models those who simply look good on terrain and in conditions that do not challenge them.

How This Section Is Organized

Traditionally, treatments of ski technique have focused on maneuvers, organized by skill level. First we learn how to perform a snowplow, then a stem turn, and so on. That layout does not engender an understanding of how skiing works. It compartmentalizes skiing into maneuvers and skiers into ability levels. How many skiers have you known who described themselves as a "parallel skier" or a "stem turner"?

Figure 5.1. Katja Seizinger, winner of two World Cup overall titles, seven World Cup discipline titles, and numerous Olympic and world championship medals, is one of the best all-around skiers of the 1990s.

The skier may have some idea of *what* she is supposed to do, but seldom knows *why*. What little depth a skier gains from this approach is convoluted and full of special cases. Our approach will be different.

This exposition is organized according to the movements we make to control the snow's interaction with our skis and ourselves. These movements are divided into the following categories:

* Movements that control the fore and aft distribution of pressure on the skis, to control the ski's self-steering effect and the skier's ability

* Up and down movements to control the overall force between the snow and the skis, to regulate how much of an effect on our motion the snow will have

* Movements that edge and flatten the skis, to control the lateral force from the snow and the ski's self-steering effect

* Movements that turn the skis, to adjust their steering angle

* Lateral movements over the skis, to balance against the reaction force from the snow

Each of these basic modes of movement accomplishes different purposes. Every particular skiing situation calls for the skier to produce a certain combination of effects. That combination of effects is accomplished by a specific combination of movements in each of the basic modes.

CHIP STRAIT

Most skiers ski as if they could walk and chew gum at the same time only if they synchronized the opening and closing of their jaws with the up and down movement of their feet. These skiers always move backward as they move up. Or they always move forward as they edge the ski. Or they always lean toward the inside of the turn as they flex. They have deeply ingrained combinations of basic movement patterns that work in basic, simple situations.

One of the secrets to becoming an expert skier is learning to move independently in each of the basic modes. The truly accomplished skier is able to mix and match movements as dictated by the situation. She can, for instance, edge the ski at an aggressive angle while moving her fore-aft balance toward the ski's tail, where a less adept skier is likely to let the ski flatten.

Alignment

There is another category of skiing movements that cuts across those described above. We make certain movements not to have a direct effect on the skis, but to align our body segments so that the bones and muscles work as effectively as possible. These movements bring into play those muscles that are most effective for the situation at hand. Often, one of these movements applies to more than one of the major categories defined above.

Alignment also applies to equipment. Boots, especially, can often be adjusted to improve the alignment of parts of the skier's body, both with each other and with the skis.

Learning

When you take the information and images from this book out to the ski slopes and experiment with your technique, you will do well to keep in mind some simple principles of motor learning.

* You learn best when you do things you are not yet good at. You learn least when you practice skills that you have already mastered or are within your comfort zone. Be willing to work at things you can't do well, to feel uncoordinated and uncomfortable.

* Your kinesthetic sense of your own movements is usually amplified and distorted. Hold your inside hand six inches higher, and it feels like two feet. So when it comes to performing a new movement, you always feel like you are doing much more than you actually are.

* You will learn a movement pattern best by pushing your body to the extremes of the pattern. Whenever you are trying to develop a movement, you should exaggerate it far beyond what you feel is about right. You must learn what it feels like to do too much of something, as well as too little.

✱ You learn new skills best in simplified environments that are not too challenging. If, for example, you are working on up and down movements to improve your mogul skiing, start by learning the movements on smooth, easy terrain. Not until you have the movements perfected should you go into deep bumps.

Kjetil Andre Aamodt and the Attacking Vikings

Norwegian Kjetil Andre Aamodt catapulted to the top of the World Cup in 1994, and has since proven to be one of the best all-around skiers of the 1990s, with one overall and four individual discipline World Cup titles, as well as five Olympic and six World Championship medals to his credit. A tough competitor, he is a threat in all events. The entire Norwegian team, who call themselves "The Attacking Vikings," is remarkably strong and deep, with numerous Olympic, World Championship, and World Cup champions in its current ranks. Aamodt, Lasse Kjus, Finn Christian Jagge, Ole Christian Furuseth, Hans-Petter Buraas, and Tom Stiansen are among the elite of ski racers. Any one or more of them could appear on the podium of any given race. Aamodt, as well as the rest of the Norwegian team, take an eclectic approach to training. They place an emphasis on versatility, well-rounded athleticism, strong fundamental physical skills on skis, and the ability to respond spontaneously to the unexpected. Gymnastics is a fundamental part of the physical education program of the Norwegian schools—and the ski team does *a lot* of gymnastics. This training practice is reminiscent of the legendary Ingemar Stenmark, whose training regimen included riding unicycles and walking on slack-ropes.

Two years ago, Aamodt and his father, who is also his coach, released a video showing Aamodt training. Much of his time on skis was spent doing a wide variety of unique and sometimes unusual exercises that bore little resem-

OLLE LARSSON

blance to high-end skiing, but stretched his balance, coordination, and body control to extremes. This presents an interesting contrast to the preferences of many junior racers in the United States, who would rather spend all of their on-snow time running through courses, and who must be pried from the gates by their coaches and forced to go free-skiing. They would do well to study the Attacking Vikings.

Fore and Aft

Thomas Sykora.

When the distribution of pressure shifts fore and aft on an edged ski, its self-steering behavior changes. Shifting pressure forward on an edged ski increases its self-steering effect, making the turn tighter. Shifting pressure toward the tail reduces the effect, broadening the turn.

We want to begin the control phase of most turns with at least a bit of extra tip pressure, because this makes the ski turn more sharply. In the completion phase, on the other hand, we want the ski to stop turning, so we often shift the distribution of pressure back to the middle or even the tail of the ski.

When a good skier makes a fore-aft movement, as often as not it is made to keep the fore-aft distribution of pressure on the skis constant. Imagine skiing off a packed trail into untracked snow. Your skis will slow considerably when they hit the loose snow, and if you make no anticipatory adjustment, your center of gravity will continue moving faster than your skis. An anticipatory forward movement of the feet prevents you from literally falling on your face.

Mogul skiing presents similar challenges. Dropping over a bump into the trough, you must press forward to avoid being left on your heels. Approaching the next bump at the end of the trough, you must prepare for skiing into the next mogul by pushing your feet ahead (figure 6.1).

Figure 6.1. Tami Bradley of Canada moves fore and aft in anticipation of the terrain.

Because of the virtual bump (discussed in chapter 4), a sharply carved turn demands similar adjustments. Just to maintain a consistent distribution of pressure over the ski, you must move forward at the beginning of the turn and back through the end.

Three things determine the distribution of pressure fore and aft on the ski:

* The ski's design

* The location of your center of gravity fore and aft in relation to the skis

* Whether your leg is pushing against the front or back of the boot

Moving Fore and Aft

Ask most skiers to move from tip to tail on their skis, and they wave their bodies to and fro. This is how their bodies have learned to control fore-aft balance from a lifetime of standing in shoes on surfaces that give them reliable friction: by moving their centers of gravity back and forth over their feet, which do not move. See figure 6.2.

When you are standing on something slippery, like skis on snow, there is a better way to make most fore-aft adjustments: by sliding your feet to and fro under your body (figure 6.3). The primary action happens in the ankles.

Since your skis, boots, bindings, and lower legs are much less massive than your torso, arms, and head, you can make adjustments more quickly and precisely by moving your feet than by moving your upper body. Controlling your fore and aft balance

Figure 6.2. In most non-skiing situations, people adjust their fore-aft balance by moving their upper bodies back and forth over their feet.

Figure 6.3. The expert skier controls pressure on the ski fore and aft by moving his foot under his body. A good indicator of where on the ski the pressure is fore and aft is the most forward spot under the ski from which snow is displaced. In the first frame, snow is spraying out from under the ski's fore-body, well toward the tip. In the second frame, no snow comes out from under the forebody: it sprays from the middle of the ski back.

with your feet also helps segregate the movements at your major joints to specific functions. The ankles are reserved for fore-aft adjustments, while flexing and extending at the knees, hips, lower back, and shoulder are reserved for vertical movements. (More on this in chapter 7.)

The Basics

Start from a flexed stance that places your center of gravity over the middle of your feet, with your ankles bent slightly so that there is no pressure against the front or back of your boots. To shift your balance forward from this neutral position, flex your ankles. Think of pushing your knees forward, or drawing your feet back. As your shins start to press against the tongues of your boots, the boots act like levers to increase the shift in pressure toward the tips. To shift pressure toward the tail, straighten your ankles. Think of pushing your feet forward. But move only your feet! Whatever you do, do not rock your body backward. Once your calf muscles have started to press against the backs of your boots, the pressure will shift quickly toward the tails.

The key point is to control the pressure as much as possible by bending and straightening the ankles only (figure 6.4). Of all the joints in your body, the ankles have the greatest effect on your fore-aft balance. Increasing the flex in the ankles by 10 degrees, for example, moves an average person's center of gravity forward by about half a foot. The knees, hips, and shoulders are used mostly for moving the center of gravity up and down in a straight line.

And remember, when the going gets tough and precise fore-aft control is called for, the expert skier drops to a low stance.

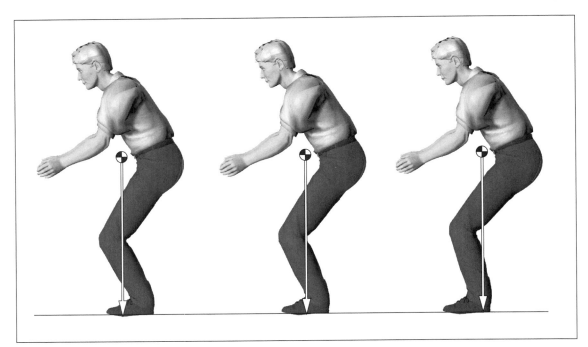

Figure 6.4. Expert skiers control their fore-aft balance by moving their feet back and forth underneath their bodies.

Boot Leverage

Your ski boots aren't shoes. They are your skis' handles. The higher and stiffer your boots, the more responsive the skis will be to small movements of your legs.

Pressing sharply against the front of your boot will put a shot of pressure on the ski's forebody. Unless it is accompanied by a movement of your center of gravity toward the tip of the ski, it will be short-lived. The back of the boot provides leverage on the tail of the ski and support that enables the skier to pressure the tail quickly without getting out of balance (figure 6.5).

Be careful when you pick your boots. To ski in the stiffest boots requires great finesse and ability, and you should be especially careful not to buy boots that are too stiff in the front. You will ski better in a boot that is a bit too soft in the front than one that is too stiff.

Finding the Skis' Neutral Point

Every pair of skis has an optimum fore-aft neutral spot, dictated by a combination of design factors. Giant slalom skis tend to favor a ball-of-the-foot neutral point, while slalom skis tend to prefer a stance centered over the arch. More forgiving skis have a wider range over which they respond well, while more demanding skis are less tolerant.

The following exercise, which instructors call *pivot slips*, is the best way I know to find a ski's neutral point. I use it often as a warm-up exercise, and to get acquainted with a new pair of skis or boots. I suggest making it the first thing you do whenever you demo a pair of skis. Start off down the fall line on a gentle slope or road. Once under way, swivel your skis back and forth 180 degrees, flat on the snow, without your body's path deviating from the fall line. In other words, try to turn your skis like windshield wipers. See figure 6.6.

Use your feet to turn the skis, keeping them flat on the snow. The skis should brush lightly against the snow, but never grip or catch.

Figure 6.5. Alberto Tomba uses the cuff of his boot, front and back, to control the distribution of force fore and aft on his skis.

You will likely need to make adjustments, both up and down and fore and aft, to find just the right stance. Every pair of boots requires a slightly different amount of bend at the ankles, knees, and waist. Different skis have different neutral points fore and aft.

Alberto Tomba

Alberto Tomba burst onto the World Cup scene in 1987, winning five races, and quickly became one of the mostly closely watched skiers in the world. Tomba's personality has drawn as much attention as his skiing, making him the most recognized skier internationally since Jean-Claude Killy.

Tomba is big for a slalom skier: not particularly tall, but massive. In fact, he is probably the biggest slalom skier to have had consistent podium-level results on the World Cup circuit. Because of his size, he must ski with a very quiet, well-disciplined upper body, otherwise small movements would result in large shifts in his balance. One way he achieves this is by always keeping his hands at the same level above the snow, mirroring each other in their movements.

Perhaps the most recognizable characteristic of Tomba's style is his overall stance, which is lower than that of most of his rivals. From this posture, he executes big fore-aft excursions by thrusting his feet to the outside in the initiation, driving his shins into the front of his boots at the start of the control phase, and thrusting his feet forward as he moves through the transition into the next turn.

The manner in which he hugs the snow with controlled, coordinated movements of his arms and legs is no doubt due in part to the influence of his technical mentor and personal coach of several years, Gustavo Thoeni. Thoeni, the Italian who dominated slalom and giant slalom racing in the mid-1970s and was the most sophisticated technician of that era, has clearly had his effect on Tomba. Thoeni is now the director of the Italian men's national team.

Alberto Tomba has been an enduring institution on the men's World Cup circuit for ten years. For much of that time, he was the man to beat in slalom

© TIM HANCOCK

and giant slalom. Indeed, whenever it looked like his star had faded, he would win yet another race. As of the end of the 1997–98 season, he had won 50 individual races. The only man to win more is the incomparable Ingemar Stenmark, who holds over 90 wins.

Beyond his athletic contributions to the sport, Alberto Tomba has been the best media ambassador the World Cup has ever seen. He is colorful, outgoing, and loves media attention. While some complain that his antics occasionally look like they belong more to the world of television wrestling than ski racing, he has done more to promote ski racing worldwide than any racer since Stein Erikson.

Figure 6.6. Pivot slips. The skis pivot back and forth while the skier's center of gravity continues in a straight line. This exercise teaches the skier where the skis' neutral pivot point is, fore and aft.

Fore-Aft Balance

When most people take up skiing, they are unaccustomed to standing on slippery things like skis. Their bodies have learned to balance against the considerable friction that has been under their feet all their lives.

Nowhere is this demonstrated better than at the top of the beginner slope, where novice skiers unload from the chair lift for the first time. Most fall over backward because they intuitively expect friction under their feet. Seeing that they are about to stand up on a slight slope (the unloading ramp), they assume a stance that anticipates a friction force pushing back up the slope on them. When that friction fails to materialize, they are left out of balance. Their expectation is shown in figure 6.7a; their reality is shown in figure 6.7b. The force diagrams in figures 6.7b and c show that for a person on a slope, the force of gravity can be resolved into two components: R_n, which acts perpendicular to the person's supporting surface, and R_s, which is trying to make him slide down the hill. In figure 6.7a, the force of gravity, G, acting on the person, is opposed completely by the reaction S from the ground. S is the resultant of the normal reaction force of the ground, S_n, and the friction force S_f. Figure 6.7b shows a person in the same stance, but on skis. The friction force S_f has disappeared, and S is the only force pushing back on the skier. R_s is an unbalanced force that accelerates the skier forward. The skier's musculature is unable to support him against the snow's reaction force acting behind his feet, so he falls over backward.

The experienced skier adopts the stance shown in figure 6.7c, which positions the center of gravity so that S acts through the skier's feet, rather than behind them. R_s is still an unbalanced force, and still accelerates the skier forward, but the skier is positioned so he can support himself. The lesson is this: the skier's fore-aft balance point has little to do with the slope of the hill, because the hill is slippery. The skier's fore-aft balance point is found by drawing a line from the center of gravity to the ski, perpendicular to the ski's base.

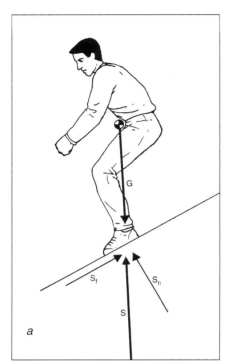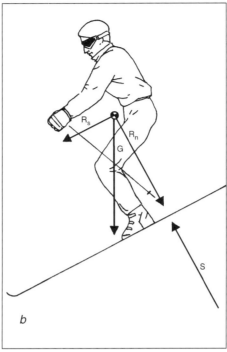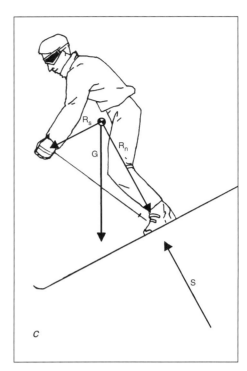

Figure 6.7.   The skier must compensate for the absence of friction.

Because alpine boots are fixed so solidly to the skis, the skier's base of support is expanded dramatically forward and back. The skier can recover from lurching forward or sitting back in a way that would otherwise not be possible. Nordic skiers, with free-heel equipment, on the other hand, have no such advantage. Instead, they make turns in the Telemark stance (see figure 6.8), with their feet split fore and aft, to lengthen their base of support.

Synchronizing Fore-Aft Movements With the Phases of the Turn

The different phases of each turn require different distributions of pressure over the ski, fore and aft. You will want to start the control phase of a typical turn with pressure forward (figure 6.9). Early in the control phase, you want the ski to start turning, and you want the snow to start making you turn, too. For this to happen, you must get the snow to exert some force on you. At this point in the turn, however, you don't have a lot of force to work with, because gravity and centrifugal force are not usually lined up. Take another look at figure 4.9. To get the most out of the force available to you, you apply it to the ski's forebody.

As you proceed through the control phase, gravity and centrifugal force become more aligned, giving you more force from the snow with which to work. To maintain a constant radius of turn, you must shift pressure to a stiffer part of the ski.

Figure 6.8. Telemark turns give the free-heel skier fore-aft stability. The fore-aft split of the feet provides a fore-aft base of support similar in size to that of an alpine ski boot in a fixed-heel binding. This is especially useful in the inconsistent snow conditions found in the back country.

Figure 6.9. Although Thomas Sykora pushes his feet forward through the transition between these two turns, he begins the control phase of the turn to the right with pressure well forward on his outside ski because his center of gravity travels a shorter line than his feet.

So, as the control phase progresses, you shift pressure off the forebody toward the middle or tail of the ski.

As the control phase ends and you want to complete the turn, gravity and centrifugal force are aligned, and you have lots of force acting on you. But you want to make the ski stop turning if you can, so you shift pressure yet farther back on the ski. A World Cup racer will often finish a turn with pressure so far back that the front half of the ski will be off the snow.

I have just made some statements that may appear to be at odds. First, I said that you want to enter the control phase of the turn with pressure on the forebody of the ski. Then I said that you want to finish the turn farther back on the ski. Since the end of one turn often melds seamlessly with the start of the next, wouldn't the finish of one turn leave you in the wrong place on the ski, back, as you enter the next turn?

Not necessarily. As your upper body enters the turn, it follows a path that goes to the inside of that traveled by your feet. During this initiation phase, the skis are turned to their initial steering angle. This puts your center of gravity farther forward over the ski than it was at the end of the preceding turn. Just how far forward it will be is determined by the angle of its trajectory to the path of the feet, the initial steering angle in the new turn, and how much you draw your feet back as your skis engage the snow. See figure 6.10.

Figure 6.10. Since Ylva Nowen's upper body travels a shorter line than her feet, she is balanced forward in the last frame of this sequence, even though she begins the turn with a forward thrust of her feet.

7

Up and Down

Few skiers move up and down with sufficient amplitude for great skiing. Few can move their centers of gravity straight up and down. Few have the finesse to prevent unwanted changes in overall ski–snow pressure, moderate them smoothly when desired, or pop the ski against the snow with sufficient force when that is the right thing to do. Most couple their too-small vertical movements with balance shifts that compromise the rest of their technique.

Moving up and down in concert with the snow and the dynamics of the turn is the mark of a fine skier; extending your own vertical range and precision is one of the simplest and biggest steps you can take on the road to becoming one yourself.

Why Move Up and Down?

We move up and down for two reasons: to control the magnitude of the reaction force the snow exerts on us, and to position our body segments so that they can most effectively achieve their tasks within the turn at any given instant.

Seeking Efficiency

Some things in skiing are best done standing tall, and some are best done deeply flexed. Other things are best done in between.

Standing tall shifts support of your mass from the muscles to the bones. It also gives muscles that have been working hard the chance to relax and flush out muscular waste products that may have built up in them.

Flexing to an athletic stance secures your balance by lowering your center of gravity. It also puts your legs in a posture that uses more powerful muscles to manipulate the ski than does a tall stance.

Seeking the Perfect Force From the Snow

The total amount of force acting between you and the snow determines how much of an effect the snow will have on your motion. If you have just passed over a bump and your skis are light, you will not be able to turn or slow down, because the snow cannot push on you. On the other hand, you can easily pivot your skis for the same reason.

At any point in a turn, traverse, or straight run, you want the snow to exert a particular amount of force on you. Sometimes you want a lot, sometimes you want a little—it all has to do with the particular place you are in the particular turn you are making. If you do not move up and down at all, the contour of the snow and the virtual bump will combine to exert changing forces on you throughout the turn. Your task is to add to or subtract from these forces by flexing and extending to achieve the amount of overall force you want.

When going straight down the hill, you are usually interested in keeping the total force from the snow constant. If there are bumps in your path, you flex and extend to negate their effects. When turning through big moguls, you usually flex at the end of the turn to reduce the upward force the mogul would otherwise exert on you. Once having crossed the crest of the bump, you extend to maintain some ski–snow pressure. The larger the bumps, the more amplitude and precision you need. In both situations, you try to move up and down in synch with the snow to keep your center of gravity from being displaced up and down.

Beginning skiers make movements that create only small changes in ski–snow pressure. They ski in simplified environments where only small pressure changes are imposed by the terrain, and they make turns that generate only small forces and no discernable virtual bump. As they progress through intermediate ability stages, skiers keep the environment simple, but learn to deliberately change pressure from ski to ski, modulate the overall pressure on their skis, and make turns that generate greater forces.

By the time skiers have reached an advanced level of ability, they have learned to make many movements to deal with anticipated and potentially disruptive pressure changes due to terrain and the dynamics of the turn. It is fair to say that good skiers make at least as many movements to prevent or reduce changes in the force from the snow as they make to create them.

Experienced mogul skiers, for example, prevent unwanted increases in overall pressure and forward shifts in its distribution as they ski into bumps by pushing their feet forward slightly and flexing their bodies. (Figure 7.1.)

Accounting for the Virtual Bump

Intermediates first start to feel the virtual bump when they start to link turns and get a feeling of rhythm. They quickly learn to like the lift and bounce they get when they link turns. At this point, they learn to time their own up and down movements to coincide with the ups and downs of the virtual bump. Their up movement and the rise of the virtual bump complement each other.

This happy synergy works well for most skiers. For the expert making sharply carved turns, though, the combination of the two can simply be too much. Extending at the same time you ski into the virtual bump at the end of the turn can be like lifting off a mogul. Now you must shift the timing of your vertical motion. Instead of extending with the bump at the end of the turn, you compress to absorb it, then extend into the middle of the next turn to maintain as much engagement between the skis and the snow as possible. See figure 7.2.

What we are talking about here is a phase shift. The cycle of flexing and extending shifts its timing as the turns get carved more and more aggressively.

To maintain contact with the snow when carving sharp turns, you must flex and extend as though you were skiing moguls, as Kristinn Bjornsson does in figure 7.3. Throughout the turn's initiation phase, you must

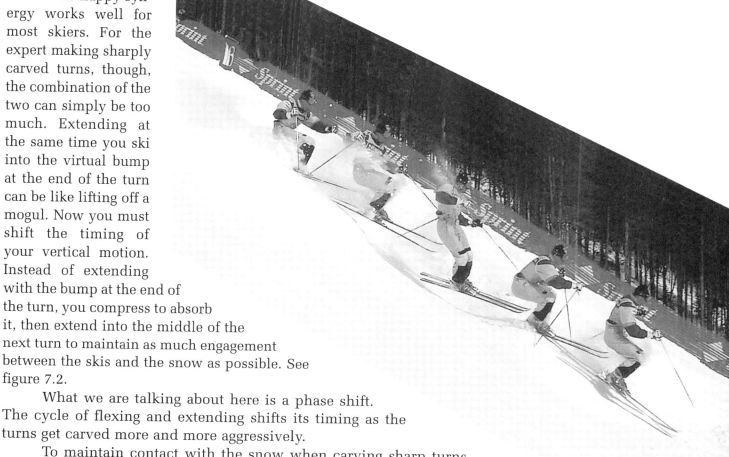

Jonny Moseley.

Figure 7.1. Jonny Moseley.

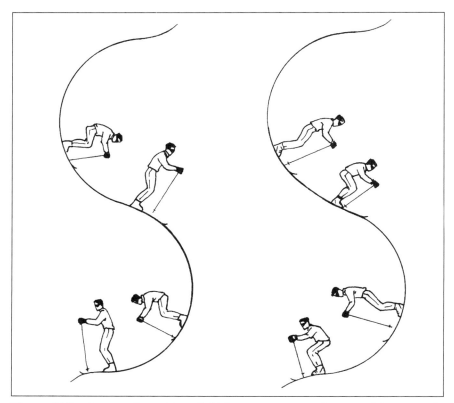

Figure 7.2. Intermediate skiers (left) learn to augment the virtual bump with their up and down movements, moving up with the bump. Experts (right) have learned to reduce the virtual bump's effect by shifting the phase of their up and down movements so that they flex as the bump comes up.

Figure 7.3. Kristinn Bjornsson, linking two sharply carved turns on a smooth slope, flexes through the transition between the turns to absorb the virtual bump. Even though Bjornsson flexes, his center of gravity is projected upward, producing an up-unweighting. This young Icelander skied out of the 49th start position to place 3rd in this race, the 1997 Park City World Cup slalom, with two exceptional runs, winning by over .6 seconds.

actively extend to keep the skis engaged with the snow. The snow's reaction force in the completion phase becomes so great that, unless you deliberately absorb it, you will be launched out of the turn just as if you had skied over a bump.

What Do Up, Down, and Vertical Mean?

These three words are so basic to our vocabularies that we assume they always mean the same things to all people. But what does *up* really mean? *Up* is the direction your supporting surface pushes on you. For a person standing at the side of a ski trail, this is the direction the trees point. For this person, up and down make conventional sense—they are aligned with gravity. As you ski by in a turn, however, you sense a different up and down. For you, the line on which these opposing directions lie is tilted toward the center of the turn (figure 7.4). It is aligned with the force from the snow pushing on your skis. You have no way of sensing where gravity alone is pointing, other than by looking at conventional vertical objects, like trees. Every other sense in your body responds only to the effect of the snow's force, which is a combination of its reaction to your weight and the centrifugal force of the turn.

Whenever we use the terms *up*, *down*, and *vertical* in this chapter, they will be from the skier's private frame of reference. It is all you have to go by when you are skiing. More important, it defines the category of fundamental movements we address in this chapter.

Figure 7.4. A skier's sense of up and down is determined by the line along which the reaction force from the snow acts.

Moguls

You may have noticed there are more photos of mogul skiers in this chapter than anywhere else in this book. The reason is simple: moving up and down is the most important movement pattern in mogul skiing. Skiing through moguls without moving up and down is like driving a car without suspension on a bumpy road.

To ski moguls well, you must be able to extend and compress your entire body in concert with the shape of the snow, so that your center of gravity barely feels the bump. If you don't, the shape of the snow will toss you and slam you. The reaction force from the snow will swing wildly, making your turns hard to control and jeopardizing your stability. The bigger the moguls, the bigger the problem.

Put simply, the single most important skill for skiing advanced moguls is the ability to move up and down through a long range of motion without your balance changing in any way. Not forward and back. Not to the inside or outside of the turn.

The first key is keeping your hands where you can see them: well out in front of your body and level, especially when you are flexing deeply to absorb a bump. As soon as one hand drops lower than the other, or falls to the side or behind you, your balance will shift to the side and back.

Think not so much of your body moving up and down, but rather of your *feet* moving up and down under your body, so that they conform to the snow while your center of gravity moves along in a straight line. As your feet come up, reach forward with your hands and feel your knees come up into your chest. If you find yourself getting bucked around, try loosening the top buckle of your boots to free up your ankles.

Another key is remembering to extend in the middle of the turn. You must do this for two reasons. First, to keep your skis in contact with the snow so you can have some control in the middle of the turn. Second, and most important, to give you a starting place from which you can flex. Many skiers remember to flex, but forget to extend. With every turn they get lower and lower, until they bottom out.

The third key technical ingredient in mogul skiing is a reliable pole plant. Convince any expert skier to descend a field of big moguls without his poles, and you will see a different skier going down the hill. Without the enhancement to his lateral balance that the pole provides at the end of the turn and through the transition to the next, the skier must be very conservative and cautious. He is likely to lean into the hill, because he cannot afford to make the error of being too far to the outside. He will stem and perhaps rotate a bit to initiate his turns because he can neither get torque from the pole plant nor can he effectively use anticipation (discussed in chapter 8).

Leg rotation augmented with anticipation and a blocking pole plant are the turning forces to be used. Knee angulation is the principal edging skill. A particularly important aspect of knee angulation in moguls is the ability to flatten the skis in the middle of the turn. A skier often needs to do this to adjust her line in mid-turn—feathering the edge and making the ski slip, either as a whole or just the tail—to avoid a rock or adjust the direction of the ski to fit the trough.

When skiers first learn to ski in moguls, they use the up-unweighting of the small bumps to help them start their turns. These skiers will often add their own extension to increase the up-unweighting. This makes pivoting the skis easy. When the moguls get bigger, though, this tactic is disastrous. The phasing of the flexion and extension must shift. Wait until you reach the end of the turn to flex, and whatever you do, do not extend until your feet have passed over the bump and begun to drop into the trough.

One common problem is falling back and into the hill. Nine times out of ten, this is due to dropping your uphill hand in the completion phase of the turn. Throughout the end of the turn and the beginning of the next, you must keep your uphill hand at least as high as your downhill hand, and reach with it across your downhill ski.

Another common problem is losing contact with the snow in the turn's initiation phase. Either you are neglecting to extend as you enter the turn, or your flexion and extension are out of phase with the moguls.

Passive and Active Flexing

In most circumstances, the expert skier flexes passively at the knees and waist by relaxing the muscles of the thighs, buttocks, and lower back, letting gravity pull the center of gravity down and the snow push the feet up. Aggressive skiing in deep moguls and sharply carved turns often confront you with such large and rapid potential increases in the force from the snow that you must actively pull your upper body forward and down to moderate those forces and stay in balance (figure 7.5). If you do not pull your upper body forward, gravity will not pull it forward and down fast enough to compensate for how quickly your legs are being pushed up, and you will end up on your heels.

The abdominal muscles and hip flexors do the work of pulling the trunk forward and the legs up. You often must pull your torso obliquely as you pull it forward, across your skis toward the outside of the turn. This brings the oblique abdominal muscles into play. Indeed, you might walk away from a day of skiing deep moguls feeling as if you had spent the time doing sit-ups.

Active flexing is part of a movement pattern named *avalement*, from the French word meaning "to swallow." Georges Joubert, the great French ski coach,

Figure 7.5. Donna Weinbrecht extends in the middle of the turn, then actively absorbs a large mogul. Notice how far she folds at the waist, and how low her hips get. Yet, her center of gravity is never behind her feet. Weinbrecht is the most successful American competitive skier of all time with 5 World Cup mogul titles, an Olympic gold medal, 2 World Championship medals, and 46 World Cup victories.

was the first to identify and analyze this movement in the late 1960s, when he saw Jean Claude Killy perform it spontaneously in certain situations. Joubert then made it a key technique in his training regimens, which produced numerous successful racers internationally. The movement pattern is more important today than ever.

Whether you flex actively or passively, the relative articulations at your major joints are the same. The amount of bend at the knees, waist, and so on should be the same. Think of it in the same way as negotiating a corner in a car. Whether you have power steering or not, you need to turn the wheels the same amount.

People watching a world-class mogul skier will often remark that the skier's knees and back must take a pounding, because they see a sharp compression of the body as the skier encounters each bump. These skiers do not take nearly the beating you might think, because those motions of the body are usually deliberate and proactive. The skier is actively snapping the body into a flexed posture in anticipation of the bump and avoidance of the force it could exert on her. Viewed from the side, you can see that the skier's feet move up and down, but her center of gravity follows a much straighter line.

Unweighting—Reducing the Force From the Snow

The terms commonly used to describe increasing and decreasing the overall ski–snow pressure (the magnitude of the snow's normal force) are *weighting* and *unweighting,* respectively. Subjectively, the words may be compelling, but technically they are misnomers. A skier's weight may change when he eats a big lunch, but it does not change when he flies off a bump into the air. What changes is the magnitude of the snow's reaction force pushing on the skier. A skier feels light when he lifts off a bump because the reaction force goes away. Conversely, the skier feels heavier when he skis into a dip because the reaction force increases. Technical inaccuracies notwithstanding, I will use the terms *weighting* and *unweighting* with their conventional meanings, because the words make sense to skiers.

The initiation phase of many turns requires some pivoting of the skis, which is facilitated by unweighting movements. These movements reduce the force acting between the skis and the snow.

Until recently, unweighting has been a central maneuver taught by all systems of ski instruction. As the slopes we ski on have become more manicured, and our skis easier to turn, focus has shifted to other skills. This is unfortunate for two reasons. First of all, to ski well in many situations still requires unweighting. Second, it was in learning to unweight that skiers have, historically, learned to move up and down properly—a skill all good skiers still need. Skiers are, in general, more static on their skis than they were 20 years ago, and I believe this is one of the reasons.

Unweighting comes in two main flavors: up-unweighting and down-unweighting. Both can be produced by the skier, variations in terrain, the virtual bump, or combinations of the three. How and when the force changes between the skier and the snow depends on the direction and timing of accelerations of the skier's center of gravity in the vertical direction. See figure 7.6.

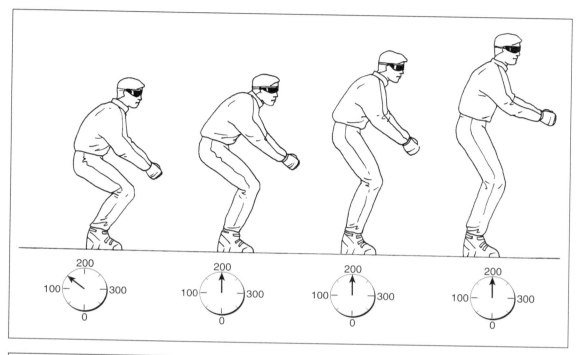

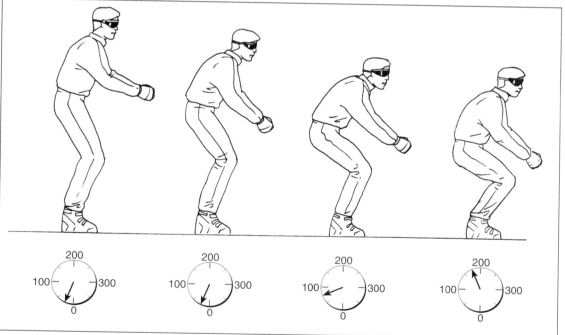

Figure 7.6. As the skier extends upward, there is increased pressure under the skis. Once the upward acceleration ends, the skier is "light" until he slows his ensuing downward acceleration.

Up-Unweighting

Up-unweighting (figure 7.7) always starts with the center of gravity being pushed and accelerated upward, away from the snow. When the upward force decreases or goes away, the center of gravity's upward motion is slowed by gravity, and the force between the skis and the snow is reduced. As the center of gravity falls back toward the snow, the force remains reduced until the downward motion of the center of gravity is slowed and stopped.

A basketball player going up to block a shot provides a good example of up-unweighting. During the push off, force under the feet increases. Once the player stops pushing upward, he feels light. This feeling lasts until he lands on the ground again, at which point he feels increased force against the floor. For a brief moment, that force will be greater than his normal weight, due to the extra force the floor must exert on him to slow his center of gravity's descent.

The force that accelerates the skier's center of gravity upward comes from the snow. In classic up-unweighting, this force comes in response to the skier pushing down on the snow to extend. Skiing into and over a bump can do the same thing. Even if the skier flexes to absorb the bump, this usually only serves to reduce the upward acceleration the bump causes, but does not eliminate it entirely. A skier of average height wearing properly adjusted boots cannot flex much deeper than about 18 inches. That is, in moving from a fully extended stance to a fully flexed one, the feet and center of gravity move no more than about a foot and a half closer to each other. This means the skier cannot absorb a bump taller than 18 inches without her center of gravity being pushed upward. The subsequent unweighting is therefore still an up-unweighting, because it begins with an upward acceleration of the center of gravity.

Figure 7.7. Up-unweighting.

Down-Unweighting

Down-unweighting starts with the center of gravity accelerating toward the snow. If you ski over a drop-off or simply relax quickly from a tall stance, you experience a down-unweighting. There is no initial upward acceleration of the center of gravity. The surface supporting your center of gravity simply disappears, and it accelerates downward. While it accelerates, the force under your skis is reduced. Remember the Roadrunner cartoons? When Wile E. Coyote ran off the edge of a cliff, he experienced a profound down-unweighting (followed by an unpleasant reweighting).

These definitions of up- and down-unweighting may seem unusual. The definitions are based on the motion of the skier's center of gravity, not the relative motions of her various body segments. According to them, for instance, the skier can experience an up-unweighting when she is flexing.

Many skiers assume that if their bodies are flexing through the transition between two turns, they must be using down-unweighting. But it is the motion of the center of gravity, not the flexing or extending of the body, that differentiates up-unweighting from down-unweighting. Only if the unweighting begins with a downward acceleration of the center of gravity is it a down-unweighting (see figure 7.8).

Figure 7.8. Down-unweighting. In the third frame, Katja Seizinger snaps into a low, flexed position. This unweights her skis and allows her upper body and feet to cross paths.

Comparing Up-Unweighting and Down-Unweighting

Up-unweighting and down-unweighting each have their strengths and weaknesses. The main advantage of down-unweighting is that it can happen instantly. No preparatory upward acceleration during which the overall pressure against the snow actually increases is needed.

The primary advantages up-unweighting has over down-unweighting are its potentially longer duration and the superior control that the skier can exercise over its length and intensity. If you were to drop a tennis ball from your hand, it would be "unweighted" only until it hit the ground. The length of down-unweighting you can impart to the ball is limited by your height. If, on the other hand, you tossed it upward and let it drop, the tennis ball would be light for a longer time. The length of the up-unweighting is limited only by how hard you can throw the ball.

Recall that from a completely extended posture, a person of average height can drop his center of gravity about a foot and a half by quickly relaxing the muscles of the lower back and thighs. The resulting down-unweighting lasts only as long as it takes the center of gravity to fall that distance. For a drop of 18 inches, this is about .3 seconds. A person performing an up-unweighting, on the other hand, can achieve reduced pressure between the skis and the snow for a much longer period, if desired. The pressure is reduced from the time the upward acceleration of the center of gravity ends until the downward acceleration ends.

Let us assume that an up-unweighting projects the center of gravity just another four inches farther above the snow than it would have started in a down-unweighting. In this case, the skier will be light almost twice as long.

Terrain Unweighting

Terrain unweighting is a phrase commonly used to describe unweighting produced by bumps or drops rather than the skier's muscles. It can be either up-unweighting or down-unweighting.

When the slope suddenly falls away, you experience a down-unweighting, even though you might extend to maintain some pressure on the snow. Conversely, a skier skiing into a bump will experience an up-unweighting if he does not flex rapidly and deeply enough to prevent his center of gravity from being projected upward. See figure 7.9.

At the intermediate level, skiers learn to use the shape of the snow itself to their advantage for starting turns. From then on, all skiers start a large percentage of their turns on bumps, from tiny lumps just a few inches high to mammoth moguls.

Figure 7.9. A small mogul can provide just enough up-unweighting to make turn initiation easy. When the moguls get bigger, the skier must work to reduce this effect.

Any such terrain feature will induce an up-unweighting. In their first forays into small moguls, skiers learn to augment the bumps' unweighting effects with extensions of their own. As the bumps get bigger, though, they threaten to unweight the skier too much, and the skier must learn to reduce the moguls' effect.

The expert mogul skier's goal is, in fact, to negate as much as possible any effect the bumps would have on his center of gravity's motion.

Rebound

Rebound is a type of up-unweighting common in short, crisp turns. The technique demands a sharp, clean edge set at the end of the turn with an abrupt increase in the snow's reaction force. The sudden force from the snow and accompanying deceleration of the skier's feet produce two effects that cause the unweighting.

The first is a "rubber band" effect of the thighs, buttocks, and lower back muscles. To get the sharp increase in pressure needed for the edge set, you allow your center of gravity to fall toward your feet, then catch it with a quick contraction of those muscles. When the contracting muscles catch the falling mass, they stretch a bit, then recoil, tossing your center of gravity back upward.

The second effect is like a pole vault (see figure 7.10). The box in which the pole vaulter plants his pole is below his center of gravity. The reaction of the box to the pole and the vaulter redirects his center of gravity into a circular arc with the box at its center.

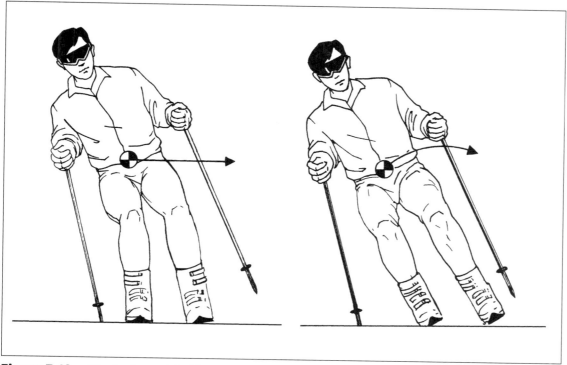

Figure 7.10. The "pole vault" effect. When the skier makes a sharp edge set and the feet stop, the skier's body will continue moving. If the legs and midbody are held rigid, the center of gravity will be projected upward as it moves laterally.

When a skier sets his edges, the snow exerts a force on the skier similar to the one exerted on the pole vaulter. The resulting upward redirection of the skier's momentum results in an up-unweighting, which the skier feels as rebound (see figure 7.11). Contrary to common belief, the skis themselves do not contribute appreciably to rebound. Compared to a skier's weight, they are simply not stiff enough to provide much of an effect.

Uncoupling Up and Down From Fore and Aft

We move up and down on skis for different reasons than we move fore and aft. Up and down movements regulate the total amount of force the snow exerts on us, while fore and aft movements control the skis' behavior in response to that force. Yet most skiers cannot move independently in those directions. They have deep-rooted couplings between their vertical and fore-aft movements. Some move forward with every downward flexion and backward with each upward extension. Every possible combination of entrenched patterns can be seen out on the mountain.

To ski with great versatility, you must be able to control independently these two interactions with the snow. You must be able to control overall force through long vertical movements without disturbing its distribution fore and aft. Likewise, you must be able to move forward or backward on the skis while keeping the total force against the snow constant.

Figure 7.11.   A rebound turn.

One of the best ways I know of to tell great skiers from not-so-great ones is to watch them make large turns through moguls. This requires the skier to move up and down completely independently of where they are in the turn, and without disturbing their fore-aft balance. See figure 7.12.

Much of a fine skier's finesse and versatility comes from his ability to make vertical and fore-aft adjustments independently, appropriate to the situation. Independent control over the overall pressure on the skis and its distribution fore and aft enables the expert to ski in response to the terrain, rather than imposing his

Figure 7.12. Making a good long-radius turn in a field of moguls requires the skier to conform with the shape of the snow, by moving up and down through a long range without her fore-aft or lateral balance being affected.

preprogrammed movement patterns on the mountain in cookie-cutter turns. Many skiers can make one or two sorts of turns well enough to get down just about any slope without looking foolish. But the true expert can adapt his movement patterns at will to produce the effect he chooses for the situation at hand.

If you can isolate the movement of your center of gravity as shown in figure 7.13, you can control the overall force and its fore-aft distribution independently. Your body is composed of segments that pivot around joints, though, and articulating at any single joint moves the center of gravity in an arc. The challenge is to combine these rotary movements to move your center of gravity in a straight line up and down.

Consider the piston in figure 7.14. It is driven by links that, like your body segments, move in circular arcs around pivot points. Yet it moves up and down in a straight line. The skier must coordinate rotary movements about the major joints in much the same way to move straight up and down (figure 7.15).

The major joints we have to work with for moving both vertically and fore-aft are the ankles, knees, hips, lower back, and shoulders (figure 7.16). Your ankles move you fore and aft. That is it. And they have very limited range in ski boots. The knees, hips, lower back, and shoulders must work together like the links driving the piston to move your center of gravity straight up and down. None of these joints move your center of gravity purely up and down or forward and backward.

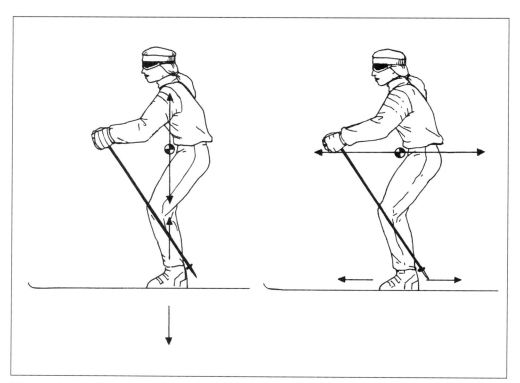

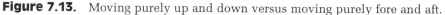

Figure 7.13. Moving purely up and down versus moving purely fore and aft.

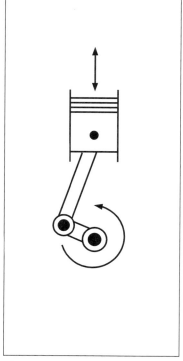

Figure 7.14. A piston moves in a straight line through coordinated rotary movements.

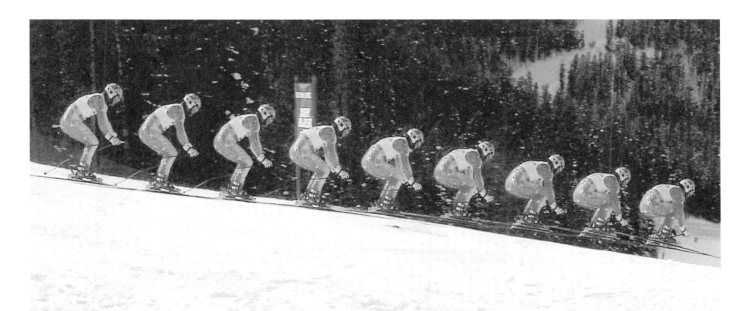

Figure 7.15. Tommy Moe absorbs a large roll at 70 mph. Flexing at the knees, hips, and lower back, his center of gravity moves in a straight line, directly along the resultant acting on it. His balance does not change fore and aft. Notice that the bend in his ankles does not change, and that his hips do not stay over his feet. His center of gravity stays over his feet, and that is what counts. In the fifth frame, Moe's feet come up off the snow. This indicates he is actively flexing, pulling his legs up and torso forward and down.

Learning the Ratios

Most everyone can move straight up and down wearing a pair of sneakers. But because they are designed to restrict ankle movement, ski boots change everything.

When people are not wearing ski boots, which is most of the time, they move up and down using coordinated movements at the ankles, knees, hips, and lower back that their bodies have deeply grooved from years of experience. When these same people buckle into a pair of ski boots, they lose the free use of their ankles, and their bodies are at a loss. Try to bend the ankle, and the boot stops you. Try harder, and it puts leverage on the ski's forebody, shifting pressure forward. Straighten the ankle past a certain point, and the back of the boot shifts pressure toward the tail.

To move straight up and down and accurately control the overall force from the snow, you must flex and extend with very little ankle movement. You must learn a different combination of relative articulations at the knees, hips, lower back, and shoulders than you use when wearing sneakers.

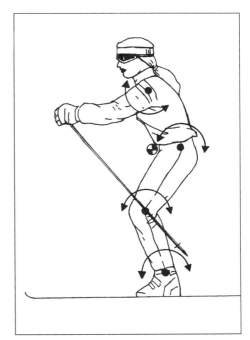

Figure 7.16. How movements at major joints affect the skier's center of gravity.

Bend too little at the waist, and the center of gravity moves down and back (figure 7.17a). Bend too much at the waist for the amount of bend at your knees, and your center of gravity moves down and forward (7.17b). Drop your

Figure 7.17a. This skier demonstrates a common problem. She starts off centered over her feet, but as she moves down, her center of gravity moves back. To compensate for the movement of her hips moving toward the tail of her skis, she needs to bend forward more at the waist as she flexes.

Figure 7.17b. Moving down and forward is another common problem. In particular, the skier bends his ankles as he flexes, both moving his center of gravity forward and levering on the tip of his ski with his boot.

Figure 7.17c. The third common vertical motion problem is moving up and back.

arms straight down while flexing, and your center of gravity will move back. Straighten too fast at the waist for the amount of straightening at the knees, and your center of gravity moves up and back (7.17c). And so on.

The combinations of articulations that work for you are specific to your body, because of the relative lengths and weights of your lower legs, upper legs, hips, torso, and arms. Other factors are your ski boots, because of their forward lean, and your bindings, because they may affect the forward lean of your boots.

The expert skier's body has learned the right articulations by making hundreds of thousands of turns (figure 7.18). Your body can learn them that way, too, but there is no guarantee that it will unless you train it right.

Start by practicing on a hard, level floor with your boots buckled tightly. Move up and down through as long a range as possible, paying close attention to your fore-aft balance. Close your eyes. How far can you flex before you lose your balance backward? Reaching up and forward with your arms will help. Practice moving through as long a range as you can until the movement pattern feels comfortable.

Now put on your skis and head for an easy slope. With every turn you make, move up and down through that long range of movement. Exaggerate! Do not let your vanity keep you from doing something you know looks funny. You learn a movement pattern best by pushing your body to the extremes of the pattern, and this one is no exception. After a run or two on something easy, you are ready to ski wherever you like, but you must exaggerate your vertical motion for at least a couple of full runs.

Figure 7.18.   In one-tenth of a second, Jesper Ronnback goes from being completely extended to being flexed in the lowest position possible while maintaining perfect balance. This movement demands great coordination of articulations at all major joints.

Considering Boot Stiffness

The difference between your ankle movement in ski boots and street shoes brings us to a topic of paramount importance: picking and adjusting boots.

The following advice is directed primarily at skiers who are looking at boots at the high-performance end of the rack. Lateral stiffness is good. The more the better, usually. Stiffness in the front is another story.

It is easy to be tempted into buying boots that are too stiff in the front for you. Because the hotter the model, the stiffer the boot, and most of us want to be hot. If the stiffness is adjustable, fine. If it is not, beware. And keep in mind that ski boots are stiffer outside in the cold than they are in the ski shop. You are almost certainly better off in a boot that is a bit too soft in the front than one that is too stiff. You can make your selection of most other boot design parameters based on fit and style, but to find the right forward flex you must consider factors that are seldom discussed in ski magazine tests or by boot fitters.

The principal discriminants you should apply are:

∗   Your personal morphology. If you are relatively heavy in the hips or lower torso, consider a softer boot. Such a physique makes forward lean adjustment critical, and at the same time difficult. Slim hips and broad shoulders will allow you more options.

∗   Your skiing ability. Unless you are a true expert skier with the experience to know what you like, stay away from the stiffest racing boots on the rack. Looking cool in the lift line is slim compensation for looking like a buffoon on the hill. Don't let me scare you, though. A boot that is mushy in the front or well below your ability level will hold you back.

*   The type of skiing you intend to do. If you intend to spend your time cruising, skiing fast, or skiing in big moguls, a softer forward flex will work better for you. Many ski racers use softer boots for downhill than for slalom and giant slalom, and many mogul competitors ski in softer-flexing boots. If you ski mostly on hard snow or have a predilection for short, quick turns, more beef in the front of the boot is helpful. Fast skiing presents the skier with rapid changes in terrain and snow texture. Unless the skier is very attentive and accurate in his movements, these changes will cause the skier's legs to press against the front or back of the boot unexpectedly. Dramatic shifts in fore-aft pressure result, making the skiing erratic and jeopardizing the skier's stability.

Mogul skiing is much harder in boots with limited ankle flexion. Each time the skis run into a bump, the tips will rise, and the skier must push the feet forward a bit to keep from loading up against the fronts of the boots. When the skis start into the trough, the tips drop, and the skier must make sure that her calves do not press hard against the backs of the boots.

Boots that are stiff in the front and back facilitate short, quick turns, but require technical finesse. Such a boot enables the skier to apply sharp, quick pressure to the tip at the start of the turn's carving phase. This helps bend the ski's forebody into sharper steering angles, facilitating the start of the turn. Moving through a short range of motion at the ankle, the skier can then quickly shift pressure toward the tail of the ski to complete the turn.

Skiing well with such a boot in a wide range of conditions is challenging, however. The performance boost they give you on hard, smooth snow may or may not be worth the difficulties they present in other conditions.

Figure 7.19. Forward lean is a crucial but often ignored design feature.

Considering Forward Lean

This critical attribute of boot design is, unfortunately, almost universally ignored or misunderstood by consumers and boot fitters alike. Proper forward lean (figure 7.19), though, is critical for maintaining fore-aft balance, and is more critical the stiffer your boots are in the front.

Forward lean refers to how far forward from a vertical line the boot's cuff is pitched. Boots have forward lean so that the skier's center of gravity can stay over his feet while he flexes and extends vertically through a large range. Too little forward lean will cause the skier to lose balance to the rear when flexing deeply (figure 7.20), and is a far more common problem than too much forward lean. Too much forward lean may

Figure 7.20. If Jesper Ronnback's boots did not have enough forward lean, he would not be able to flex to this low a position without his center of gravity getting behind his heels, putting him irrecoverably out of balance.

require the skier to adopt a posture that is too low for comfort, too upright at the waist for smooth vertical motion, or too far forward on the skis. World-class racers and mogul skiers typically ski in boots with enough forward lean to allow them to flex very deeply.

To see the effects of forward lean for yourself, buckle your boots up tight and find a hard, level floor. The top buckle, in particular, must be as tight as it would be for serious skiing. Now, see how low you can crouch before you lose your balance backward. Be sure to keep your hands out in front of you at shoulder level, reaching as far forward as possible. See figure 7.21.

Now repeat the exercise with a one-inch-thick board or book under the toes of your boots. This has the effect of reducing the forward lean of an average-size boot by around 5 degrees. You should find the depth to which you can crouch reduced noticeably. Try the test again with the board under your heels. You should find it much easier to get to a low position.

Figure 7.21. Testing the effects of forward lean changes.

The critical parameter that changes in these tests is the angle of your lower leg to the floor. This angle compensates for the restriction your boots place on the ankles' range of motion.

Figure 7.22 shows the effect of a change in forward lean on the skier's center of gravity. The only difference is the forward lean in his boots, shown by the two different angles of his lower legs. The flex at the knees and hips are the same. On the left, the skier is in balance, but on the right, the skier whose center of gravity is behind his feet, is not. If he were not on skis and bent at the angles he is in on the right, he would fall over.

How much forward lean should your boots have? With your boots flat on the floor (no lift under the toe or heel), you should be able to get your hips down at least to the level of your knees. If you cannot get that far, you cannot flex that low to absorb a bump without losing balance to the rear. Your boots need more forward lean. If you can easily get your rear end much lower than your knees, you may have more forward lean than you need.

If you need more forward lean and your boots do not have a forward lean adjustment (not many do), try inserting some flexible but firm material between the back of the liner and the boot cuff. (Trail maps work well for experimenting, as in figure 7.23.) Try at least 1/4 inch to feel the effect. A piece of flexible plastic or rubber is a more permanent solution.

Take this test as a starting point to gauge how much lean your boots have. Experiment with the setting until you find the spot that works best for you when you are out on the hill skiing. Just make sure you test each setting in situations that demand a long range of vertical motion, such as moguls. Skiers who rarely venture into moguls or who ski in soft boots might be all right with less forward lean than the above test suggests. Those who like skiing deep moguls or whose boots are very stiff in the front might want a bit more.

One last thing to keep in mind: forward lean angles published by boot manufacturers do not provide meaningful comparisons between brands or models. This is because the standard practice in the boot industry is to measure forward lean as the angle between the cuff of the boot and a line perpendicular to the boot's footbed, rather than the sole. So the published forward lean numbers for boots with different footbed ramp angles cannot be compared. Also, since the skier's tibia may not be at the same angle as the boot's cuff, depending on the musculature of the calf, qualitative comparisons are difficult based simply on the boot's measured cuff angle.

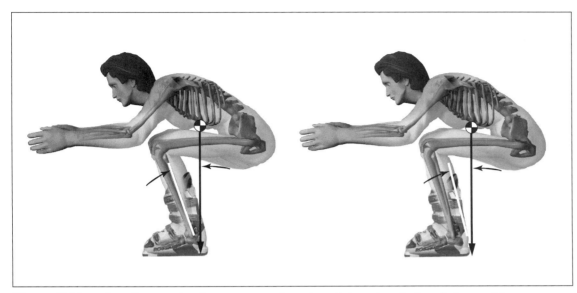

Figure 7.22. The effect on the skier's center of gravity of changing the boot's forward lean.

Special Considerations for Women

Most high-performance boots are designed for men, and do not account for important physiological differences between men and women.

Since women tend to carry more of their weight in their hips and upper thighs than men, their centers of gravity are more apt to move behind their feet as they flex. This suggests that many women would need boots with more forward lean built into them. But the characteristics of women's calves complicate things. They tend to extend farther down their lower legs than those of men, and are often thicker. As a result, the calf muscles take up more space in the cuff of the boot. With more muscle between the bones of the lower leg and the back of the boot cuff, a typical woman's lower leg will be pitched farther forward than a man's, giving her effectively more forward lean.

Figure 7.23. Trail maps are great for on-the-hill forward lean augmentation.

If the shape of your calves pushes your lower leg too far forward or your boots are just too tight around your calves, try placing a quarter- to half-inch heel lift inside your boot. (For test purposes, folded paper napkins work quite well.) This will lift the calf muscle farther out of the boot, making the cuff fit more as it would around an average man's leg. Such a lift will also allow you to flex your ankles more without bearing on the front or back of the boot.

Once your boots fit to your liking around your lower legs, adjust the overall forward lean so you can get your hips down to the level of your knees without losing your balance backward. Do this with the method mentioned previously.

Many manufacturers design models of boots especially for women. Some of these, unfortunately, focus more on feminine aesthetics than physiology, and may even have design parameters that make skiing more difficult for women. For example, some women's models have little forward lean, the designers evidently thinking that women are more interested in standing very straight in the lift line than skiing well on the slope.

Heel Lifts

Placing a heel lift inside the boot can help solve many boot problems, but it does little to change the fore-aft position of the skier's center of gravity, and does not solve fore-aft balance problems in the same way as adjusting the boot's forward lean.

The main effect of putting a heel lift inside the boot is to make the boot effectively shorter (figure 7.24). The top of the boot no longer comes up as high on your leg, and your calf muscle, because of its taper, no longer fills the cuff of your boot as tightly. The net effect is that you have more freedom to flex your ankle: a positive effect for many skiers.

Inserting a heel lift inside the boot will move your center of gravity forward, but not much. All other things being equal, placing a quarter-inch heel lift in a boot with a 5-degree ramp angle and 18 degrees of forward lean will move your center of gravity forward by about 1/10 inch. By comparison, increasing the forward lean to 20 degrees in the same boot will move your center of gravity forward about 1/2 of an inch—15 times more.

Raising the heel inside the boot will also make the boot fit tighter on the instep and change the alignment of the ankle bones with the cups that are built into the liner and shell.

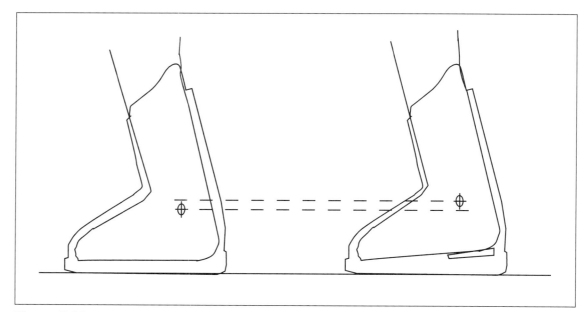

Figure 7.24. Putting a heel lift inside the boot effectively makes the boot cuff lower.

8

Turning the Skis

efore *you* can turn, the *ski* must turn.

If you have enough room, and the terrain is gentle enough that you don't pick up too much speed, you can make the ski turn itself from the very beginning of the turn, never twisting it yourself. Such turns, however, constitute a minority of those made by a skier on any given day. Terrain and turn shape dictate that the skier start most turns by pivoting the skis at least a bit. The steeper the slope and the sharper the turn, the greater the initial steering angle needed. Extreme skiers on extreme slopes often pivot their skis 90 degrees or more at the start of the turn. World Cup slalom and giant slalom racers begin many turns with significant steering angles, as Thomas Sykora does in figure 8.1.

You can redirect your skis in three ways:

1. Shift pressure well forward and make the tail slip

2. Use internal muscular forces, putting a twisting force on the ski

3. Use a pole plant to get the snow to put a twisting force on your entire body

In the 1950s and 1960s, many instruction systems differentiated themselves by which of the techniques in the second category they promoted. For years the official French school promoted upper body rotation, while the Austrians espoused counter-rotation and heel thrust. The controversies died down in the 1970s as people came to realize that all top-level ski racers used essentially the same techniques. The differences in national ski schools from that time have centered mostly on how to teach those movements.

Figure 8.1. Thomas Sykora initiates this turn by pivoting his skis more than 40 degrees.

87

Hermann Maier.

Leg Rotation

The preeminent technique used today to turn the ski, and the preferred technique for most situations, is twisting one or both legs at the hips (figure 8.2). When instructors talk about "turning your feet," this is what they mean. It is used in skiing maneuvers of all levels, from gliding wedge turns to dynamic parallel turns.

Ski instructors and coaches call this technique *braquage* (pronounced *bra-KAJ*), a French word that literally means "steering." It was first analyzed and described by the French ski technician Georges Joubert and the great ski champion Jean Vuarnet in their 1966 book, *How to Ski the New French Way.* The book and technique had a huge, worldwide impact on ski instruction, and the technique has been with us ever since.

If you turn both legs at the same time, or there is weight on both of your feet when you twist your leg inward, your upper body will remain motionless, and you can turn your skis without disturbing your balance.

If, on the other hand, you twist only your outside leg inward and lift your inside foot off the snow, your upper body will react by turning a bit toward the outside. This sets your upper body into a countered position, ready for hip angulation early in the turn. This is a technique racers have used for decades. See figure 8.3.

Leg rotation is one of those key techniques of skiing that is, unfortunately, not obvious to many self-taught skiers. The intuitive movement for most people is to twist their upper bodies and hips in the direction they want their skis to turn—movements that have counterproductive side effects. Turning the leg in the hip, to

Figure 8.2. Martina Ertl turns her skis with leg rotation, turning the upper legs turning in the pelvis. Neither the hips nor the torso move appreciably.

Figure 8.3.   Martin Hansson of Sweden lifts his inside (right) foot as he rotates his outside leg inward to initiate this turn. As a result, his upper body and hips turn slightly toward the outside of the turn.

the degree that a good skier does it, just does not seem to show up in any other sport, and that is probably why people do not naturally do it on skis.

To feel the movement for yourself, sit on the very edge of your chair with your feet and knees about six inches apart. Now, without moving your heels, twist your right leg so that your right big toe touches your left foot, and your right knee touches your left knee. This movement is the essence of leg rotation. You may feel as if you are twisting your knee, but in truth you are twisting your femur in your hip.

A straight leg cannot exert as much turning force on the ski as a bent one, so this technique is most powerful when performed from a flexed, athletic stance. For a better approximation of true leg rotation, stand up and try drawing a large *C* on the ground with one foot, as shown in figure 8.4. This will show you the range of motion possible in the hip.

There are several reasons why leg rotation works so well. Rotating the leg usually rolls the ski on its edge, too, combining the increase of steering angle with an increase in critical edge angle—usually a desirable combination. Leg rotation is also powerful. With it you can produce large torques, and produce them for several seconds, much longer than any other rotary technique. Leg rotation also works well because it allows you to manipulate your skis with your legs alone, leaving your upper body to balance against whatever forces are acting on you. It imparts no angular momentum to you, and because it involves the movement of relatively little body mass, leg rotation does little to disturb your balance and stability.

Anticipation

This is a technique used mostly in linked short turns. Although inklings of the movement pattern can be seen in pictures of skiers from the 1950s and earlier, it became commonly visible in the skiing of world-class ski racers in the mid-1960s. To this day, it remains a fundamental element of advanced short-turn technique, and is sometimes referred to simply as *windup/release*. See figure 8.5.

Figure 8.4. Drawing foot arcs in the snow will help you feel the movement of leg rotation.

Figure 8.5. Donna Weinbrecht's pole plant and anticipation cause her skis to turn when her feet reach the crest of the mogul where the tips and tails are not restrained by the snow.

From the fall line to the crossover into the next turn, your legs wind up under your torso, which continues to face down the fall line. The resulting twist in your body through the hips and lower back stretches a number of muscles, some of them large. When the skis disengage from the snow, either by unweighting or flattening at the crossover point, those stretched muscles seek to shorten, realigning your legs with your upper body (figure 8.6). A blocking pole plant is frequently used to stabilize the upper body, so that all the realignment takes place in the legs.

The muscle tension created by the windup is not a strong source of torque for turning the skis, but supplies enough to be useful in turns where the skis are unweighted, especially when augmented by a well-planted pole.

Anticipation enhances leg rotation, and that is one of its greatest benefits. It places the hips and legs in a posture that provides the maximum range and power for leg rotation. In addition, the muscles that are stretched in the windup phase are the same ones that are used for leg rotation. Because a muscle will develop its maximum contracting force when it is first extended to about 120 percent of its resting length, the windup of anticipation enables the skier to perform a more powerful leg rotation. Finally, anticipation coordinates well with the high degree of hip angulation and countering that are often effective in the completion phase of short, linked turns.

Figure 8.6.   Due to the anticipation developed at the end of the previous turn, this skier's body unwinds in the air, and his skis swing toward the fall line. Notice also how his upper body turns slightly toward the outside.

Torque From the Pole Plant

Planted properly, your pole will do something you might not have thought it could: it will make you turn.

First, you must plant the pole at a particular angle. All great skiers, from Zeno Colo to Alberto Tomba, have always planted their poles at this angle. When the tip of the pole goes in the snow, it is always ahead of the hand that planted it. This is the critical element that enables the snow to exert a turning force on the skier (figures 8.7 and 8.8).

With the pole planted obliquely, the snow can push backward on your hand, creating a torque on your entire body. This is sometimes called a *blocking pole plant*. If the pole is planted straight up and down, the snow cannot do this. See figures 8.9 and 8.10.

Figure 8.7. The pole plant is an essential technique for applying rotary forces to the skis. To be effective, the pole must be planted at an angle, with the tip ahead of the hand.

Figure 8.8. Ylva Nowen plants her pole obliquely to initiate her turn.

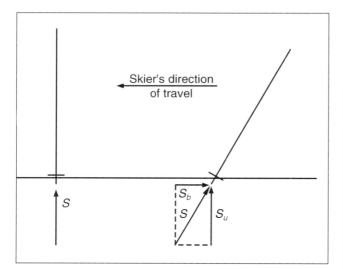

Figure 8.9. Why an oblique pole plant is important, part 1: the snow S can push only upward on the pole on the left. The pole on the right, however, also encounters S_b, a component of S pushing back on the skier's hand, and S_u, a component of S pushing up on the skier.

Figure 8.10. Why an oblique pole plant is important, part 2: The snow's force pushing backward on the skier's hand, S_t, produces a torque, T, on the skier.

This ability of the snow to apply a torque to the skier is very useful in short turns. It becomes critical on very steep slopes where significant rotary force must be applied to the skis to achieve big initial steering angles.

How much torque you want from the pole plant varies from turn to turn. Many turns, especially long-radius ones, require none at all. You can precisely and instantaneously control the amount of torque the pole plant produces by controlling the strength and duration of the contraction of your arm and shoulder muscles. The more firmly they contract, the greater the torque you will get. The longer the muscles are contracted, the longer that torque is exerted on you.

In addition to planting your pole at the correct angle, you must plant the pole solidly in the snow at the right time (figure 8.11). That is the crossover point, when your skis are flat on the snow and you have the best opportunity to pivot them. This means you have to make the actual movement of planting your pole earlier, so that it will be in the snow, up to the basket, when the crossover happens.

The two most common problems advanced skiers have with their poles is that they plant them too late and too straight. Many skiers wait until they have started the turn to plant their poles. And when they do plant them, they plant them straight up and down, instead of obliquely.

Skiers who lack an effective pole plant often compensate with some form of rotation (discussed in the next section), a rotary push off, or stemming the uphill ski. Adding a good pole plant to their tool kits can make their short turns dramatically crisper and more controlled.

Imagine grabbing the ends of a foot-long piece of garden hose and giving one end a good twist. If you now let go of both ends, they will both turn as the hose unwinds. If, on the other hand, you only let go of one end, it will turn twice as far as it did when you let go of both ends.

In the first half of the transition phase between two short turns, your legs wind up under your upper body, stretching many of the muscles in your legs and midbody. At the crossover point, when your skis go flat, are perhaps unweighted, and are easy to turn, your body responds something like a garden hose.

Just as the tension in the hose caused both ends to rotate when they were both released, your upper body will turn toward the outside of the turn when the leg turns inward. Unless, that is, your upper body is stabilized by a blocking pole plant. In that case, your upper body cannot turn toward the outside, so all the twisting force is applied to the ski.

Leg rotation, anticipation, and an oblique blocking pole plant are complementary techniques (see figure 8.12). Together, they synergistically constitute the most effective package for creating the initial steering angle for high-end, short-radius turns. And, as figure 8.13 shows, the best skiers in the world show remarkable similarity in their pole plants.

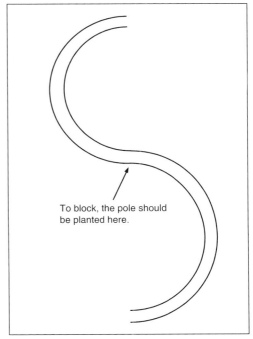

To block, the pole should be planted here.

Figure 8.11. To be effective, the pole plant should occur at the very start of a turn, or at the inflection point between linked turns.

Figure 8.12. Thomas Stangassinger uses anticipation, leg rotation, and a blocking pole plant to pivot his skis through the initiation of this turn.

Alberto Tomba

Thomas Stangassinger

Thomas Sykora

Sebastian Amiez

Michael von Gruenigen

Siegfried Vogelreiter

Finn Christian Jagge

Kjetil Andre Aamodt

Figure 8.13. A gallery of pole plants. Eight of the top fifteen slalom skiers in the world plant their pole in the same way in the same turn on a steep, icy slope. Note, too, the position of each skier's inside hand.

Upper-Body Rotation

Upper-body rotation is a classic technique for pivoting the skis and creating a steering angle. It is intuitive and powerful. Many books on skiing from the 1940s, 1950s, and earlier have beautiful black and white photographs of expert skiers rotating their way through billows of untracked powder. This was the technique of Hannes Schneider's Arlberg school and the French school of Emile Allais. Schneider is generally credited with starting the first true ski school in the Arlberg region of Austria. Allais was a great French champion of the late 1930s who went on to become the father of the French national ski school and designed skis.

These skiers swung the whole upper body—arms, shoulders, and all—into the turn. All well-rounded skiers still use this technique at one time or another. Many is the time an expert powder skier will throw off a full-on shoulder rotation to deal with a tight situation. But when skiing with skis that turn easily and snow that was groomed the night before by hundred-thousand-dollar machines, a subtle swing of the outside hand is often all that is needed to start a turn.

Upper-body rotation involves projecting some upper-body segment, such as an arm or shoulder, in the direction of the intended turn (figure 8.14). The movement is prepared with a windup of the segment, after which it is thrown in the direction of the intended turn. Once the segment has gained some momentum, it is caught by the contraction of appropriate muscles, locking it to the rest of the body. This transfers the momentum of the thrown body segment to the rest of the body and the skis as a torque.

The skis must be engaged with the snow during the windup and throw. Otherwise, the rest of the body will counterrotate in a direction opposite that of the projected body segment. For the rotation to have the greatest pivoting effect on the skis,

Figure 8.14. Upper body rotation. The skier powers the initiation by swinging his shoulders in the direction of the turn. Notice how this straightens the left side of his body, flattening his outside ski. This movement also gives his entire body angular momentum that can carry through the whole turn.

they should be disengaged from the snow at the time the thrown body segment is blocked. See figure 8.15.

To get a feel for the power and elegance of upper-body rotation, troll the used book stores in your town for ski books from the mid-1950s or earlier. You will see a technique well-matched to the equipment, snow, and sensibilities of the era, when skiing was a vigorous, adventurous, and romantic sport pursued by true outdoors people.

Powder Skiing

Skiing in powder snow is one of skiing's greatest joys. It is not difficult, either, it's just foreign to most skiers. Most otherwise advanced skiers will venture gingerly into deep snow for one or two runs, take a few tumbles, and high-tail it back to the groomed runs where they feel more confident. If they were to commit themselves to one whole day of skiing the loose stuff, they would find themselves spending the next day looking for more.

The first order of business is to dispel an old myth: that you should sit back in powder. This is most skiers' first reaction, but it is simply the wrong thing to do. Sitting back makes skiing in powder far more difficult and tiring than it should be.

Keep your center of gravity over your feet. You can make 95 percent of your turns with your center of gravity moving no farther forward than the ball of your foot and no farther back than your heel. As with most turns, you should begin the control phase a bit forward, and finish the turn a bit back. Your neutral position should be perhaps an inch or two farther aft on your skis than it is on hard snow and ice, but not more. Stay flexed at the waist and make your fore-aft adjustments with your feet, not your upper body. Try skiing with the top buckle of your boots unbuckled. This will give you more leeway with your ankles and keep you from overpowering your skis with too much pressure on the tips.

Just accept that you will fall more in powder than in other conditions. It comes with the territory, and you usually have a very soft landing.

Getting the turn started is the biggest technical challenge. Establishing your skis' initial steering angle and your body's inclination into the new turn are tough because there is so much resistance to the skis moving laterally; much more than you are used to dealing with on packed slopes. Start by initiating your turns with an uphill stem. This is the simplest, easiest, and most reliable way to start a turn in loose snow. As your speed and boldness increase a bit, start a steady, exaggerated bouncing or rhythmic up-unweighting in synch with some hip rotation to help start your turns. This will enable you to do away with the stem initiation.

As you ski faster and make tighter turns, you will get more reaction force from the snow. Now you can dispense with the hip rotation and make turns using more or less the same mechanics you would on soft, packed snow, but at a slower tempo. In particular, give yourself more time to get through the initiation and into the control phase of each turn. Patience is a virtue. You will never be able to get through the first half of the turn as quickly in powder as you can on packed snow, and so you will always pick up more speed in that part of the turn. Just remember that you will have to ski a bit faster, in general, to get the same dynamics out of a turn in powder snow than you do on packed snow, and that the forces just take longer to develop.

As for skis, choose short, wide, soft, and shaped. The advantages of a short ski (187 cm or less) far outweigh the disadvantages. In particular, they are simply easier to turn. You will be able to make turns at slower speeds with less effort, and this means you can ski with much more security in the trees, where the best snow usually is. Rarely will you reach the speed limit for a pair of skis in powder snow. Be wary of powder skis that are extremely wide (more than 120 mm at the tip) or have little sidecut. They may be nice in deep fluffy snow, but they can be a real nuisance on anything else.

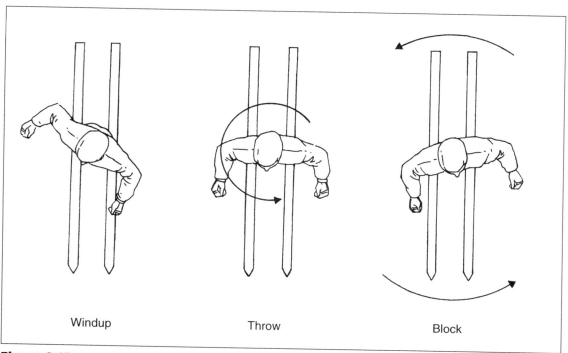

| Windup | Throw | Block |

Figure 8.15. The mechanics of upper body rotation.

Hip Rotation

In hip rotation, or hip projection as it is sometimes called, you initiate the turn by pushing your hips to the outside. This flattens your skis, making it easy to slip the tails out to a good-sized steering angle, even if they are pressed against the snow. The movement of the hips can also produce a twisting force on the skis, like upper-body rotation. The best skiers use it in certain situations, but all skiers should avoid using it methodically for all their turns.

Hip rotation is an effective and perfectly acceptable technique in loose snow (figure 8.16), particularly at slower speeds or on flatter terrain, where flattening the skis helps them move laterally through the snow. It is also occasionally useful in small doses in moguls, where feathering the edge is often desirable to help adjust the ski's line through the top half of the turn.

To begin using hip rotation effectively in powder, imagine your body is a big corkscrew, with the point between your feet, and the handle across your shoulders. Keeping flexed at the knees and waist, twist the handle of the corkscrew in the direction you want to turn. Avoid tipping your body or shoulders. Just make big torques by cranking the corkscrew straight down into the snow. It is a specialized technique, however, for special situations. When you leave the powder and crud behind, leave the hip rotation there, too.

You can get away with using hip rotation to start turns on packed snow if you then bring your hips back to the inside of the turn, to counter and angulate properly. Skiers whose boots are overcanted (discussed in detail in chapter 9) sometimes use

Figure 8.16. Hip rotation in powder snow. The subtle but powerful movement occurs in the third frame.

this tactic to get their turns going. Unfortunately, most skiers who begin their turns with hip rotation never make the adjustment, and are left facing their tips with no hip angulation. This leads to an overreliance on knee angulation, and difficulty making short, quick turns because the upper body is turning with the skis.

The Good . . .

Upper-body and hip rotation are powerful techniques. Using them, you can redirect your skis even when they are submerged in powder or crud. A subtle side effect of both techniques is that they usually flatten the skis. While this is a distinct liability on hard snow, it is an asset in powder because your skis then show a narrower profile to the snow, making it easier for them to slice sideways through it as they swing into the turn.

The Bad . . .

There are just not that many skiing situations these days requiring the oomph that upper-body and hip rotation provide. Worse, they tend to put just about every part of your body in a bad place for the rest of the turn, especially on packed snow. Because the hip moves toward the outside of the turn, you are prevented from countering and angulating at the hip effectively (discussed in chapter 9). The skis flatten on the snow, and you tend to end up forward on them. Consequently, the tails usually slip.

Great skiers can start a turn with an emergency rotation, then quickly bring everything back together for the rest of the turn, but most skiers suffer through the whole turn with the ill effects of the initiation.

Short turns are difficult using hip or upper-body rotation because your whole body picks up angular momentum. This takes some time to get going, and also some time to stop, which works against the rhythm of short turns. Also, both types of rotation make your upper body follow your skis through the turn, making short turns that much harder.

Counterrotation

This is the technique of the late 1950s and 1960s that captured the imagination of skiers everywhere, and attracted millions of Americans to the sport of skiing. Identified mostly with the Austrian school of skiing, it was a cornerstone of a system that included *heel-thrust* and the *comma position*. The pinnacle of such skiing was *wedeln*: silky trains of short, linked turns, and the narrowest feet-together stance imaginable. (*Wedeln* [pronounced *VAYD-len*] is a German word meaning "to wag," as a dog wags its tail.) This is how everyone wanted to ski.

Heel-thrust is best described as a way of making the tails slip toward the outside of the turn through careful management of the ski's critical edge angle and foreaft pressure control. The comma position, also called *reverse-shoulder* in this country, was the descriptive name for what we now call hip angulation and countering.

The theory behind counterrotation as a technique for turning the skis is this: if the skier twists the upper body strongly in one direction, the lower body (and skis) will naturally twist in the other direction. Some cited Newton's third law as validation for the theory. (Newton's third law states that whenever one object exerts a force on a second object, the second object exerts an equal and opposite force on the first. The colloquial version is, "Every action has an equal and opposite reaction.") The problem with this theory is that it only works if the snow offers no resistance to the skis turning. In other words, they must be completely unweighted. The skis themselves have sizeable moments of inertia, presenting significant resistance to being redirected, and virtually any engagement between them and the snow will prevent the lower body and skis from twisting in the opposite direction of the upper body.

Only if a skier is airborne will twisting the torso in one direction cause the skis to turn noticeably in the other direction, as in figure 8.17. We do see good skiers

Figure 8.17. This skier uses the principle of counterrotation to perform a twister. The skis turn easily because they are completely free of the snow.

instinctively use counterrotation in such situations. It is, in fact, the only technique that will turn the skis when the skier has lost contact with the snow completely. As a systematic technique for turning the skis, however, counterrotation simply does not work. It puts only a small torque on the skis, and for only an instant.

Close examination of many pictures from the 1950s and 1960s shows that skiers relied heavily on blocking pole plants and subtle hip rotations to start their ultranarrow–stance parallel turns. The apparent counterrotations generally came *after* torque was applied to the skis, their main purpose being to provide hip angulation and the fashionable, much sought-after comma position. The extremely narrow stance these skiers employed in parallel turns made any leg rotation virtually impossible, and spawned a generation of American skiers who became difficult ski school students for years to come.

9

Edging the Skis

All skiers learn early on the importance of edging skills. Ask them what they do to make their skis turn, and they shrug their shoulders. Ask them how they edge their skis, and they crank their knees in. While ski flex, sidecut, and torsion are subtleties that go forever unappreciated by most skiers, sharp edges are something they all understand.

When it comes to controlling their edges, skiers concern themselves most with making their skis hold on hard snow. It is just as important, however, to make the ski slip predictably, and to be able to change smoothly from one pair of edges to the other when starting turns in a parallel stance.

For the expert skier, controlling the ski's edge does more than keep it from slipping. Changing the critical edge angle can also change the radius of a turn in progress. We saw in chapter 3 that as the ski's critical edge angle is increased, it will hold farther toward the tip and tail. This, in turn, amplifies the ski's self-steering effect, while decreasing the critical edge angle does the opposite.

The Biomechanics of Holding

Your intuition tells you that big edge angles make your skis hold. The bigger the better. It is easy to draw this conclusion. After all, the harder you crank your knees into the turn, the better your skis seem to grip.

Your intuition is wrong. Recall from chapter 3 that for the ski to hold, it simply needs to cut a step in the snow at a right angle to the resultant of gravity and centrifugal force. In other words, you need a critical edge angle of 90 degrees or more under the midbody of the ski.

Putting the ski at that angle is the first key to making it hold. The second key is aligning your body so that you can keep the ski at that angle while you take care of other aspects of the ski–snow interaction.

Have you ever thought about how an ice skate holds? Skates are not nearly as stiff and powerful as ski boots. The ice in any rink is as hard as the worst boiler-plate a skier is ever likely to see. Yet a casual skater can describe clean arcs on a rink, while good skiers often struggle to make good turns on snow that is not nearly as hard.

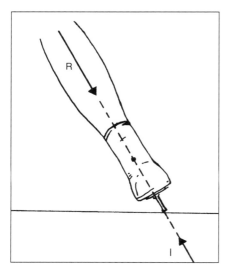

Figure 9.1. An ice skate holds well because the edge is directly beneath the center of the skater's ankle.

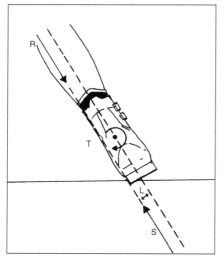

Figure 9.2. A ski's edge is offset from the center of the skier's ankle. This puts a torque on the skier's ankle, making the ski flatten and slip.

The difference lies in the relative locations of the ankle and the weight-bearing edge. The blade of an ice skate is directly under the center of the skater's ankle (figure 9.1). So when the skate is on edge, the force that the ice exerts on the blade passes directly through the center of the skater's ankle. In figures 9.1–9.4, R is the resultant of gravity and centrifugal force. I or S is the force from the ice or snow.

In contrast, the edges of a ski are offset from the center of the skier's ankle. In figure 9.2, the force S from the snow acts along a line that passes outside the skier's ankle. The distance L from that line to the skier's ankle creates a lever arm through which S exerts a torque T on the ankle. T seeks to twist the skier's ankle, flattening the ski on the snow and making it slip. The longer L is, the greater T will be.

Unless this torque is completely resisted by the ski boot and the ankle muscles, the ski's critical edge angle will drop, and if that angle gets below 90 degrees, the ski will slip.

The second key to holding, then, is to make the ski more like a skate: to get the center of the ankle as close as possible to the line along which the force from the snow acts.

The closer the center of the skier's ankle is to the line along which the force from the snow acts, the smaller will be the torque on the ankle, and the easier it will be for the skier to make the ski hold. This is why skis that are narrow under the foot hold better than wide ones. It is also why skis hold well in soft snow. As the ski is driven farther into the snow surface, as shown in figure 9.3, the snow's reaction force moves closer to the center line of the ski, making the lever arm shorter, and the torque smaller.

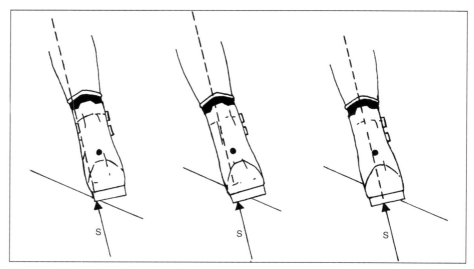

Figure 9.3. Why do skis hold well on soft snow? The ski on the left is on hard snow, and its edge does not penetrate far into the surface. The other skis, on softer snow, penetrate farther, bringing the force from the snow, S, closer to the center of the ankle.

Deborah Compagnoni.

Angulation

Angulation is the general name for a number of movement patterns that create angles in the skier's body at certain joints. These angles have two key effects: they adjust the ski's critical edge angle, and control the alignment of the ankle with the force on the ski's edge, making the ski behave more like an ice skate (figure 9.4).

Angulation comes in two major flavors: knee angulation and hip angulation. They have both been with us for a long time, sometimes under different names. Pictures of the best skiers as far back as the 1920s show both.

Knee Angulation

Technically speaking, knee angulation is a movement that brings the knee closer to the midline of the skier's body without moving the center of gravity laterally. Put in everyday terms, it means cranking your

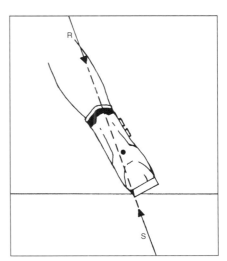

Figure 9.4. By angulating, the skier brings the ankle into line with (or close to) the force from the snow. This eliminates the torque on the ankle, enabling the ski to hold.

Figure 9.5.   Knee angulation.

knee in. This movement comes naturally to skiers. It is the movement they make intuitively when they want the ski to hold better.

We call it knee angulation because it looks and feels like you are twisting your knees (figure 9.5). Physiologically, you are rotating your femur in the ball-and-socket joint it makes with your pelvis. The knee, a hinge joint, simply cannot flex inward to any appreciable degree. The hip joints' freedom of motion and the powerful muscles that control it enable the skier to turn the leg inward while bent—to angulate at the knee.

Sit on the edge of your chair with your feet about a foot apart. Without moving or turning your feet, bring one knee over to touch the other. This is knee angulation. Notice that this movement is similar to leg rotation (figure 9.6).

The muscles used for knee angulation vary with the posture of the leg. When the leg is fairly straight, the medial rotators of the femur in the pelvis roll the ski up onto its inside edge. When the leg is bent, the femur's adductors, which

Figure 9.6.   Martina Ertl uses the similar movements of knee angulation and leg rotation in combination.

are much stronger, do the work. This suggests that you will be able to hold the ski on edge more effectively under load when you are in an aggressive, low stance.

The skier on the right in figure 9.7 is angulating at the knee. This has moved the ankle closer to the line of the force on the ski, reducing the length of the lever arm and the torque on the ankle. Once the torque is small enough that it can be resisted by the boots and ankle muscles, the ski holds smoothly.

Too much knee angulation can be a bad thing. Remember that the knee is a hinge joint, and if it is turned too far inside of the force on the ski, that force can make it bend in ways it was not meant to. Trying to absorb a large mogul with the knee cranked far to the inside, for example, can be dangerous.

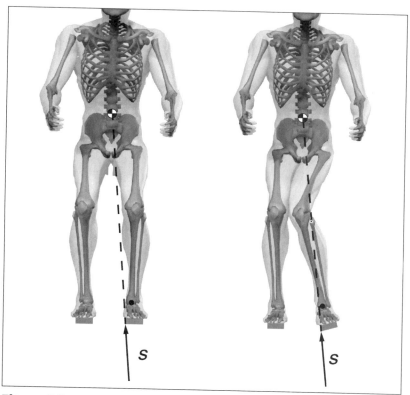

Figure 9.7. By rotating the leg inward at the hip, knee angulation brings the ankle closer to the line of action of the snow's reaction force.

ICE

Skiing on ice requires technical conservatism and steadfast balance on the outside ski.

By technical conservatism I mean that you must be careful and restrained in your movements. Small fore-aft adjustments are all you need. Big commitments to the inside of the new turn may leave you set up for more lateral force from the snow than you actually get. Look carefully where you are going, and anticipate the slick spots.

Most important, though, is to put all your weight on your outside ski and angulate at the knee and hip. Remember that most skiers do not angulate enough at the hip, so put your hips into the turn and reach out over your downhill ski with your arms and torso. Do not be afraid to come down hard on your ski when you need it to

hold. If you don't push it into the snow, your ski won't hold. Practice setting your edge from a sideslip on gentle terrain, then some short, punchy turns. Focus on your downhill ski, and if you feel the tail slip, you are too far forward. If the outside ski runs away from you down the hill, you are too far back.

Sharp, well-tuned skis are a must. Aggressive skiing on hard snow will dull a sharp edge quickly, so touch them up at least every couple of days if you ski on man-made snow or ice. Boots must be stiff laterally, tight fitting, and canted properly. If skiing with your boots tight is a little hard on your feet, unbuckle them for the lift ride up. If they are cushy and comfortable when buckled, they may too big.

Hip Angulation and Countering

Hip angulation (figure 9.8) is a movement that brings the head of the outside femur closer to the inside of the turn without moving the center of gravity laterally.

Like knee angulation, hip angulation brings the ankle closer to the line of action of the snow's reaction force on the ski. Unlike knee angulation, it does not come naturally, and self-taught skiers often lack hip angulation skills. To accelerate your progress, then, you should pay close attention to how you angulate at the hips. This is not to say that hip angulation is more important than knee angulation; just that knee angulation comes more naturally.

To angulate at the hip, you move it toward the inside of the turn. At the same time, you lean your upper body toward the outside so that your balance side to side does not change.

Figure 9.9 shows two first-seed World Cup slalom racers whose individual styles and physiologies favor different degrees of knee and hip angulation. Claudia Riegler has comparatively wider hips than Martina Ertl, and more muscle mass in her thighs and the muscles surrounding her pelvis. Ertl, on the other hand, has proportionately wider shoulders and more massive upper torso. These differences account, in part, for Riegler's greater hip angulation.

Figure 9.8.   Hip angulation.

Figure 9.9. Claudia Riegler of New Zealand (left) relies almost exclusively on hip angulation, while Germany's Martina Ertl uses more knee angulation. Riegler must bend her upper body farther to the outside of the turn to compensate for her relatively heavier and wider hips.

Countering. To be most effective, hip angulation involves a movement called countering (see figure 9.10). It is a twisting movement in the hips and lower back that aligns your body so that the most effective muscles are used for hip angulation. It is not an edging movement, per se, but without it effective hip angulation is not possible.

To counter, the skier either turns the hip toward the outside of the turn, or turns the outside leg inward. (This movement is, biomechanically speaking, identical to leg rotation.) Hip angulation now becomes a matter of bending over in the hips and lower back. This moves the head of the femur toward the inside of the turn, while the torso goes to the outside.

It is a general biomechanical principle that the strongest muscles can support the greatest loads with the most finesse. Ask a muscle to work against a load that taxes its limits, and you cannot expect the muscle to work with precision.

To angulate at the hip, your outside hip joint must move to the inside of the line connecting your center of gravity with the edge of the ski. If you do not counter, but rather face the tips of your skis while you do this, you must bend sideways in your lower back—a movement controlled by relatively weak muscles. If, on the other hand, your hip turns on top of the femur toward the outside of the turn, you move the hip into the turn by folding over at the waist—a movement controlled largely by the buttocks muscles, which are considerably stronger than the lower back muscles.

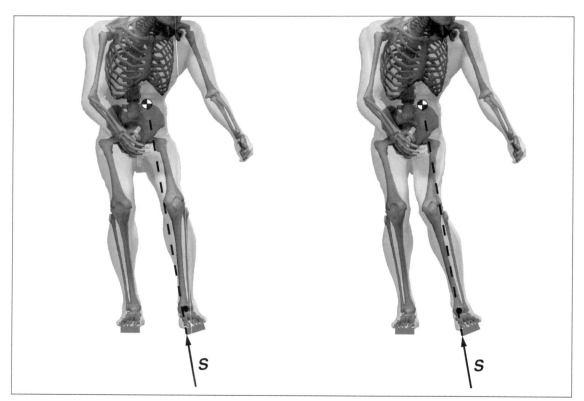

Figure 9.10. Hip angulation and countering: alone (left), and with knee angulation (right).

Moreover, moving up and down from a position of hip angulation with no countering is awkward. Many small muscles get involved, and the movement is stiff and hard to control. When properly countered, the biggest muscles in the body, the buttocks and quadriceps, do the work through the entire range of vertical motion. See figure 9.11.

At the other extreme, too much countering makes effective knee angulation difficult. The hips are turned so far that the limit of inward articulation of the outside leg is reached before the ankle is brought into line with the force from the snow.

Stefan Krukenhauser and his disciples at St. Christoph-am-Arlberg, Austria, institutionalized hip angulation and exaggerated countering in the 1950s. They used the terms *counterrotation*, *reverse-shoulder*, and the *comma position* to describe their techniques. The style of skiing they promoted demanded a lot of hip angulation, because the extremely narrow stance they affected made knee angulation difficult. This style captivated recreational skiers around the world, attracted many people to the sport, and created a generation of skiers who spent years trying to ski with their feet too close together.

Gender Differences. In general, the distribution of mass in women's bodies is different from that of men. Women carry proportionately more in their hips and less in their upper torsos. How far into the turn a skier should put his or her hips depends on the location of the outside hip joint and the location of the ankle with respect to the force of the ski. How far to the outside a skier must put his or her shoulder, on the other hand, is dictated by how much weight that hip movement puts to the inside of the turn. In other words, the upper body is put to the outside

Figure 9.11. Hip angulation with and without countering. Without countering, the skier on the right must bend sideways in a way that stiffens his midbody.

of the turn to counterbalance the movement of the hip to the inside. And since most women's hips have more mass than men's, and their shoulders less, women must usually counter and fold at the waist more than men to stay in balance while getting the same edge control.

Hip Angulation and Countering Exercises. Since hip angulation and countering are not second nature for most skiers, it pays to deliberately target these movement patterns with on-snow exercises.

Having a friend pull on your poles, as shown in figure 9.12, a–b will give you the feeling of hip angulation and countering. Pointing your uphill ski down the hill turns your hip over the femur, and reaching with your arms makes you fold at the waist—both essential elements of hip angulation.

The best exercise for developing good hip angulation and countering is the javelin turn, demonstrated in figure 9.13. The idea is simple: pick your inside ski up and point its tip toward the outside of the turn and hold it there through the whole turn. The more you can cross it over the outside ski, the better. This turns your hip to a countered position and puts it to the inside of the turn. Really good skiers can make javelin turns of just about any size on just about any terrain. It is one of the best all-around exercises I know of. The etymology of this exercise's name dates back to the mid-1960s, when Art Fuerr, a Swiss skier who was probably the first well-known trick skier, invented the maneuver for his repertoire. He named it after the model of ski that his supplier, Hart, was promoting at the time.

Practice early countering and hip angulation in medium to large turns by pushing your inside foot forward in the initiation phase of the turn while drawing your outside foot back. Then reach with both arms toward the outside of the turn, putting your hips into the turn and your shoulders over your outside foot.

Figure 9.12a. This exercise helps the skier angulate at the hip and counter.

Figure 9.12b. Pointing the uphill ski down the hill increases the skier's countering.

Figure 9.13. A javelin turn. Picking the inside ski up and pointing it toward the outside of the turn makes the skier's hip turn toward the outside putting her in a countered position.

Coordinating Knee Angulation, Hip Angulation, and Countering

Good countering and hip angulation gives you the feeling of being supported by the thigh bone. There is a sense of the body's weight riding on the head of the femur, especially in medium- to large-radius turns. This is because the strongest muscles in the body, the thighs and buttocks of the outside leg, are doing the lion's share of the muscular work. A less-than-optimal alignment enlists weaker muscles to the task, which is easy for the skier to feel.

Hip angulation alone will not bring the ankle as close as possible to the snow's force on the ski. Knee angulation is needed to finish the job (refer back to figure 9.10). As you turn the outside leg inward, a point will often come at which the ski seems to "lock" into the snow. If there is adequate hip angulation and the boots are properly canted, this feeling is a good indication of adequate knee angulation, assuming adequate hip angulation has already been established.

In small-radius turns, which usually involve significant leg rotation early in the turn, you should feel that the leg rotation blends directly into knee angulation. Hip angulation comes later in the turn, more the result of your outside leg winding up under your body than your body turning to the outside. See figure 9.14.

In medium- and large-radius turns (figure 9.15), which do not often require much leg rotation, you should turn the upper body toward the outside early in the turn to establish a countered position in the turn's initiation phase. As the ski is loaded at the beginning of the control phase, the hip will go toward the inside as the skier folds over at the waist toward the outside of the turn, establishing hip angulation. The next order of business in the control phase is to turn the knee inward to fine-tune the critical edge angle and ankle alignment until the edge is felt to be slicing the snow cleanly. Finally, in the completion phase, the skier will reduce her countering as she pushes the outside foot forward and begins the transition to the next turn, which will require countering in the other direction.

Figure 9.14.   As the skier progresses through the turn, her knee angulation increases. Since her hips do not follow her ski tips but remain facing more or less down the hill, she becomes more countered, and angulates more at the hip as the turn proceeds. Notice that the motion of the leg also produces leg rotation.

Figure 9.15. Entering a giant slalom turn, Urska Hrovat counters, turning her hips and torso toward the outside of the turn. This aligns her to angulate and balance over the outside ski in the upcoming control phase of the turn.

The Effects of Ski Design and Binding Lifters

The first skis known to have sidecut were made by Sondre Norheim in Telemark, Norway, in 1868. They were 70 mm wide at the waist. By 1970, skis had narrowed a bit. The Rossignol Strato, a premier slalom racing ski of the time, was 68 mm wide. Since then, things have changed a lot. In 1998, the Italian racer Deborah Compagnoni was disqualified from the final slalom race of the World Cup season for competing on a pair of skis 57 mm wide at their narrowest point—1 mm less than the rules allowed. Elan, the Slovenian ski manufacturer, is producing skis that are a mere 47 mm wide under the foot.

By becoming narrower, our skis have become more like ice skates. A narrower ski simply puts the force from the snow closer to the skier's ankle, meaning it is easier to make the ski hold.

Lifting the ankle farther from the edge with binding lifts (figure 9.16) also brings it closer, for a given amount of angulation, to the line of force acting on the ski. Figure 9.17 shows the effect of doubling the height of the boot sole above the snow with binding lifts. The center of the ankle, represented by a black dot, has been brought closer to the line of action of the force on the ski, reducing the torque produced on the ankle by that force. This is what skiers who use such lifts commonly describe as "increased leverage" on the edge.

The governing body of World Cup ski racing, the Fédération Internationale de Ski (FIS), has imposed a limit on how far the boot sole can be above the snow. Many racers

Figure 9.16. The plates under this binding more than double the height off the snow of the boot's sole.

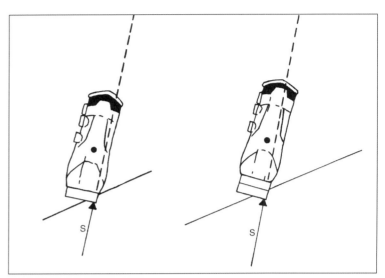

Figure 9.17. The effect of a binding lift. The center of the skier's ankle is brought closer to the line of the reaction force from the snow, *S*, making the ski hold better.

would put more lift under their boots if they could, simply because of the increased holding power this would give them. In response, boot manufacturers are making the soles of World Cup racers' boots thicker. (The thickness of the boot's toe and heel, which the binding clamps to, are not changed so that the bindings continue to work properly.)

The Look of Modern Edging

Better boots, binding lifts, and narrower skis have reduced the amount of angulation required to make most turns. These and other advancements in equipment have also enabled racers to make sharper turns, which demand that the skier balance against greater centrifugal forces. The result is an overall look of more inclination and less angulation (figure 9.18). Keep in mind, however, that the same skills and movements are needed to ski well today as they were 30 years ago. Only their relative amplitudes have changed.

Comparing racers in the late 1990s with those of the mid-1970s, we can see that in 1976, a world-class skier had to angulate more than a racer of today to get a modicum of edge hold. He had to angulate more because his skis were wider, stiffer, and straighter, and his boots were softer and lower. At the same time, the racer of yesteryear inclined into the turn much less than today's champion because he could not get the edge grip needed to support the centrifugal force of a sharper turn (figure 9.19).

Boot Canting

As boots and skis have become more responsive, they have also become more sensitive to their alignment with the skier's body segments. One such alignment is lateral canting, usually referred to simply as canting.

Regardless of how well you angulate and counter, it will count for little if your boots are badly miscanted. The lateral cant of a ski boot is the deviation of the boot's cuff from a vertical line when viewed directly from the front, as shown in figure 9.20. The angle between the two lines in the figure is the cant of the boot. Most skiers do well with boots canted between 1 and 3 degrees, but many people require settings outside this range.

Most people's legs do not rise straight up from their feet. Rather, they bow outward slightly. A boot's cant functions, in part, to conform to this, and to coordinate the ski's critical edge angle and the alignment of the skier's ankle with the force from the snow.

What if you were to angulate to your physiological limits, and the critical edge angle of your outside ski was still less than 90 degrees? You would never be able to hold on hard snow. This is the plight of grossly undercanted skiers. Try as they might, their skis will not hold because they cannot achieve a critical edge angle of 90 degrees. Moderately undercanted skiers have problems, too, because they will use most of their range of motion simply to get the ski to hold, leaving them no ability to tighten the turn by angulating more. The tails of their skis often slip at the end of the turn, and

Figure 9.18. Sarah Schleper of the United States, racing in 1997 on very hard snow. Twenty years ago this much inclination was unseen in such conditions.

Figure 9.19. Gustavo Thoeni, in 1976. Considered by many to be the most technically important skier of his time, Thoeni was the skier against which all others were measured from the early 1970s until Ingemar Stenmark's arrival on the World Cup circuit. Thoeni's influence is still directly evident today. He was Alberto Tomba's personal coach for a number of years, and directs the Italian men's ski team.

their excessive knee angulation commonly leaves them facing their tips as they go through the turn, rather than countering. Because most skiers naturally push their knee forward as they twist in, undercanted skiers also usually end up with excessive forward pressure as they go for more and more knee angulation.

An undercanted skier looks knock-kneed, especially from behind. The best times to see this are when the skier is in a straight run, or at the crossover point between two parallel turns, when both skis should change edges at the same time.

Figure 9.20. Lateral cant.

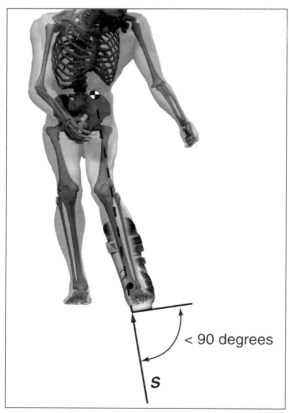

Figure 9.21. Severe undercanting. In spite of strong angulation, the ski's critical edge angle is less than 90 degrees.

Figure 9.21 depicts exaggerated undercanting. The skier will angulate to align his ankle with the force from the snow, but the ski will still slip because its critical edge angle is less than 90 degrees. The skier simply cannot make the ski hold on hard snow without excessive angulation, or perhaps not at all.

A highly overcanted skier has different problems. This person cannot make his outside ski slip without moving his knee to a bow-legged position. When going from one turn to another in a parallel stance, the skis will change edges at different times, and the skier will often ski in a very narrow stance to reduce this problem. Finally, in the control phase of the turn, the ski will engage far toward the tip and tail even when the skier is not highly angulated, making the ski hooky. If severely overcanted, the skier's ankle will be well outside the line of force on the ski all the time, even when the ski is at an aggressive critical edge angle. This puts great torque on the skier's ankle, making the ski feel choppy and chattery.

Overcanted skiers often look bowlegged and ski with their feet close together. Just as with an undercanted skier, this is easiest to see in a straight run or the transition between turns. They may push the hip out at the beginning of the turn in order to make it slip, and often make the control and completion phases of the turn with significant weight on the inside ski, since it has less of an edge than the outside ski.

Figure 9.22 shows what happens when the boot is badly overcanted. The critical edge angle is 90 degrees, but the ankle is well outside of the line of the snow's reaction force. That force will produce significant torque on the ankle, causing the ski to roll outward and slip. If the skier angulates more to bring the ankle into line with the force on the ski, the ski will be greatly overedged and will not behave well. When the skier is in a neutral stance, the ski's tip will engage the snow, causing it to turn. Extremely overcanted boots will put enough of the ski far enough past 90 degrees that its forebody and tail cannot flex smoothly, causing it to be choppy.

Your legs may each require a different amount of canting. Even if each leg is in the ballpark, each ski will behave differently if one boot is off by a degree or two. The edges will not change at the same time when starting a turn to the left as when starting a turn to the right, and one ski will turn more sharply than the other, given the same amount of angulation.

Proper canting puts the ski at the right critical edge angle when the hip, knee, and ankle are in the right place. The ski will be at a sufficiently high critical edge angle to hold and turn well when the skier is comfortably countered, the knee is comfortably angulated, and the ankle is close to the line of force on the ski. See figure 9.23a–b for examples of undercanting and overcanting.

Do you need to adjust your boots' cant? You won't know until you try. And even if the final answer is no, it is worth experimenting with cants because it will teach you something about how your edges work. You need no special equipment—just some firm snow to ski on, the willingness to experiment, and some simple materials you can find at any ski area: trail maps. They are a good size and thickness for jamming in your ski boots in just the right places to jimmy the canting. If your ski boots have a cant adjustment that is effective (many are not), you can use it rather than trail maps.

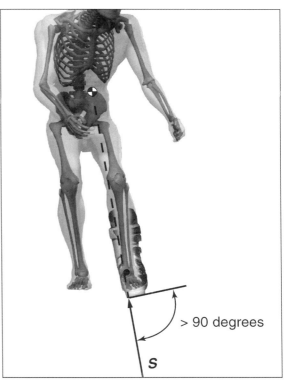

Figure 9.22. Gross overcanting puts the ski at a critical edge angle of 90 degrees or more while the skier's ankle and knee are well outside the line of action of the force from the snow.

Figure 9.23a. This skier demonstrates the look of undercanted boots.

Figure 9.23b. Here, he shows what a skier with overcanted boots looks like.

Place two or three folded trail maps between the shell and liner of each boot (figure 9.24). Put them over the inside edges of your skis to increase your boots' canting, and go skiing, starting off with some pivot slips. (This exercise is described in chapter 6.) Add a few more trail maps to each boot and try again. Then move the maps to the other side of your boots, reducing the cant, and ski some more. Try different amounts of cant in each boot, too.

After a half-day of such messing around, you should have a good idea of what canting is all about, and an opinion of what works for you. (If the snow is very soft, you might not feel much difference.) Don't worry if you seem to like different degrees of canting on each boot. This is common.

Once you know how much adjustment you want in each boot, it is time to replace the trail maps with a more durable material (rubber or plastic works well), or modify your boots or bindings. If your boots have a built-in adjustment mechanism, try using it, but don't be surprised if it does not seem to make much of a difference. Otherwise, go to a specialty ski shop and have the best boot fitter there work on your boots. An alternative is to put canting plates under your bindings. Whether the boot fitter grinds your boot soles, adjusts the cuff of the boot, or places wedge plates between the bindings and skis, the result will be pretty much the same.

One last note: if your boots are canted perfectly for you when they are brand new, they will probably be undercanted after 20 or 30 days of skiing. As the liner compresses with use, the effective cant of the boot decreases.

Custom Footbeds

Most of the force between your body and your ski boots is pushed through the soles of your feet. It makes sense, then, that your boots should fit the bottoms of your feet at least as well as they fit the sides and tops. And this is why you should seriously consider getting a pair of custom footbeds (figure 9.25) made for your ski boots. Not

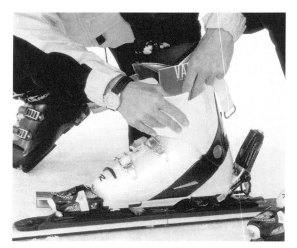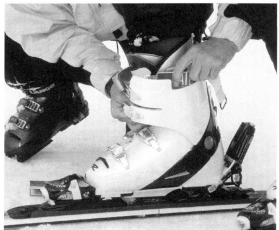

Figure 9.24. Trail maps can be used to experiment with cant adjustments on the hill.

only will your boot now fit the bottom of your foot well, your foot and ankle will be prevented from rolling, flattening, and arching as under your ski through each turn the force ebbs and flows.

Compared to how much a pair of ski boots costs, footbeds are not expensive, especially considering that a well-fitted and well-made pair of footbeds will last a long time and can be moved from one pair of boots to another. Just be careful. Get them made for you by someone who has been doing it a long time, and who makes a lot of them. If you have problems with your feet (such as very high arches, hammer toes, or

Figure 9.25. A good pair of custom footbeds will improve both your skiing and your comfort, and can last through several pairs of boots.

unstable feet), consider having a podiatrist make a pair of true orthotics for your ski boots. Although some ski shops talk loosely about making orthotics for ski boots, only a podiatrist can legitimately claim to make them.

Do not be fooled by claims that all your boot alignment problems can be solved by custom footbeds or heel lifts and wedges inside the boot. While they can help make small adjustments in the position of your ankle over the edge, they cannot change the basic geometry of your boots—the angle between your lower leg and the base of the ski—and are seldom a complete substitute for cants.

Coming to Grips With Your Boots

How much cant is optimal? The answer is different for every foot on every skier. It is possibly different for different snows, different skis, and different skiing styles. Phil and Steve Mahre reportedly changed the canting in their boots from year to year. Some very good skiers simply take their new boots out of the box and go skiing. Others tinker constantly.

There is little doubt that an accomplished skier can feel a 1-degree change in cant on hard snow. But it is not always clear what is optimum, or that there even *is* an optimum cant for any one skier. Mechanical methods can be used to check for gross misalignments and to provide a starting point, but serious skiers should always experiment with more and less canting. By doing this, they develop sensitivity to their boots and edges, and very soon become able to judge for themselves the best degree of cant in each boot. Many excellent skiers report that they can ski perfectly well with their boots set within a range of a couple of degrees. They make small adjustments in their skiing depending on the canting in their boots, but do not feel that one setting is better than another.

Do not take as gospel the judgments of anyone other than yourself. Many top-flight World Cup racers have skied in boots that some would say were overcanted. Primin Zurbriggen, the great Swiss champion of the 1980s, for example, often looked noticeably overcanted, yet he won many World Cup races and Olympic and World championship medals. Sebastian Amiez and Claudia Riegler are current examples.

The greatest danger in any cant measurement system is that the skier who subscribes to it as gospel may transfer some of the responsibility for his skiing to the measurement device and the person wielding it. Setting up your boots is something like coming back from an injury. Any athlete who has successfully recovered from a major injury knows that rehabilitation was his own responsibility. Those who shift responsibility to doctors and physical therapists do not make the same sorts of recoveries. Similarly, you do yourself a disservice if you let another person cant your boots, then ski off into the sunset believing they are perfect. No one's measurement system, regardless of how scientific or precise it may seem, is as relevant to your skiing as your own experience.

Lateral Balance

f I were to pick one aspect of ski technique that, more than any other, differentiates skiers of different abilities, it would be how they balance against the lateral force from the snow—the force that makes them turn.

Novices ski with their feet apart because their lateral balance is uncertain. At the other end of the spectrum are experts who can, and usually do, balance entirely on one ski at a time. Many skiers in between want nothing more than to ski with their feet glued together, and mess up their skiing by trying. One of skiing's ironies is that those who try hardest to ski with their feet together will usually never be able to do it on any but the easiest slopes. Skiers whose focus is on effective, functional technique will eventually be able to ski with their feet as close together as they like.

Balancing Against the Snow's Lateral Force

Back in chapter 2, I said that an object will be stable as long as the resultant acting on its center of gravity passes somewhere through its base of support. The example I used was a box that had only one force acting on it: gravity.

In a turn, both gravity and centrifugal force act on you, so the resultant on your center of gravity acts at an angle, along a line inclined into the turn (see figure 10.1). For you to be stable, that resultant (R) must still pass through your base of support: the areas enclosed by your skis. Gravity's effect on you is constant, but centrifugal force changes all the time, and so the resultant acting on you does, too. The tighter the turn, the greater the centrifugal force, and the more inclined the resultant.

If your stance is wide, you have a lot of leeway. The resultant will stay within your base of support with little effort on your part. If you want to ski in a narrower stance, your base of support will be much smaller. You will have to estimate more accurately how much centrifugal force you will encounter, and incline your body so that your center of gravity and feet are precisely aligned with the resultant.

Figure 10.1. Gravity, G, and centrifugal force, C, act on a skier during a turn. R is the resultant of the combination of the force of gravity and centrifugal force.

How much centrifugal force the turn will generate is determined by many complex factors, including the condition of the snow, the design of the ski, and the ski's steering and edge angles, just to name a few. That skiers can figure this out on the fly is amazing in itself.

An inexperienced skier does not know how much centrifugal force he will meet with from moment to moment in a turn. So he does not know where exactly the resultant force on his center of gravity will point. To provide a margin of safety, the skier establishes a wide base of support, either with a wedge or a wide-track parallel stance. The skier keeps a significant amount of weight on the inside foot and waits for the lateral force to build under the outside ski.

As he gains experience, the skier can assume a narrower and narrower stance, because he can better anticipate the centrifugal force, and hence the direction of the resultant.

Deborah Compagnoni.

Balancing on the Outside Ski

As long as I can remember, since I began skiing in the mid-1950s, instructors and coaches have exhorted their charges, "Stand on your downhill ski!" (And I am sure that they were saying it for decades prior.) Today, that advice reads, "Balance on your outside ski!" See figure 10.2.

Patrick Russel, a World Cup champion of the early 1970s, said that the most important tip he could give skiers was to work constantly from outside foot to outside foot. Marc Girardelli, the only person to have won the overall World Cup five times, and certainly one of the best skiers to ever walk the planet, has said that once you can balance perfectly on the outside ski, everything else will follow.

Why One Ski?

When the snow is hard and you want to extract the maximum grip from your skis, putting all of your weight on one ski is crucial. The force you apply to a ski can be divided into two components: one that pushes on the ski laterally, trying to make the ski skid, and another that drives the ski into the snow. (Refer back to figure 3.1.) The deeper the ski penetrates the snow, the less successful the lateral force will be in making the ski slip.

Figure 10.2. Making a hard turn at 65 mph, 1998 World Cup downhill champion Andreas Schifferer holds his inside hand up and forward to help him balance on his outside ski. Notice how much he counters to align his biggest muscles with the force of the turn.

Putting all your weight on one ski maximizes the penetrating force relative to the slipping force. As soon as you put some weight on the other ski, the penetrating force decreases faster than the slipping force, and you are at a disadvantage.

Why the Outside Ski?

Your body just works better that way. It is put together such that, when it must balance against a force from the side, it balances best on the foot that is to that side.

If I were to ask you to jump from side to side from one foot to the other, you would naturally land on your left foot when jumping to your left, then push off of that foot to jump back to your right. You would then land on your right foot and push off of it to jump to your left. In other words, you would naturally jump from outside foot to outside foot. You would find it unnatural to jump from inside foot to inside foot; jumping toward your right, but landing on your left and visa versa. Your body knows this from years of experience, and you should use the outside foot in the same way when you ski.

Steeps

When the going gets tough, the tough stand on their downhill ski and plant their pole.

Leaning out over that downhill ski at the end of the turn is as much a psychological challenge for many skiers as it is a technical challenge. All of your primal instincts tell you not to. They tell you it is dangerous. They tell you to lean back into the hill, splitting your weight between your feet. That, however, is the path of true peril. It reduces your grip, encouraging your skis to slip. It makes your downhill leg straighten, reducing its effectiveness. It makes it harder to start your next turn without stemming. The common symptoms of this instinctual response are dropping your uphill hand, straightening your downhill leg, turning your upper body with the skis, and leaning into the hill.

In short, your natural response to the situation is the wrong one, and you must train yourself to make the right one. This is the difference between being frightened and being thrilled. Both involve fear. The difference is in how you deal with it. When you are frightened, your fear determines what you do. When thrilled, you perform deliberately and correctly, while your fear rides along in the passenger seat. Being scared is no fun. Being thrilled is exciting. And while leaning out over the downhill ski can be downright frightening at first, seasoned skiers learn to enjoy it.

The key cue is keeping your uphill hand where you can see it, and reaching it out over the downhill ski at a level with, or higher than, the downhill hand. This will help keep your weight balanced over the downhill ski. It will also keep your upper body facing down the hill while your skis complete the turn, giving you hip angulation, countering, and anticipation.

An ultrareliable pole plant is your best friend here. It will let you lean out over your downhill ski and into the void, but hold you up in case you overcommit. Without it, you cannot really get over the downhill ski, because you cannot afford to pay the price of overcommitment.

These turns are all initiation and completion. You can afford to spend little time in the control phase, as you will pick up speed there. If you find yourself picking up speed with each turn, you need to pivot the skis farther in the initiation. Leg rotation, anticipation, and that rock-solid, oblique pole plant are the keys to getting the skis around.

All the Time?

Just about. Unless the snow is very soft, you will almost always make a better turn if all your weight is balanced on your outside foot, especially in the control phase. Even when the snow is very soft, a dominant outside foot usually works very well. Deep powder skiing is the only place I know where even weighting is desirable.

Since most skiing situations favor balancing entirely on the outside ski, it is worth working at. The times when it is most important are the times it is hardest to do. Steep terrain, hard snow, and high speeds all demand absolute commitment to the outside ski. These are also the times when your emotions are most likely to drag you toward your inside ski.

Where Are Your Hands?

Most skiers pull their balance away from the outside ski by dropping their inside hand. Watch the inside hands of world-class skiers, particularly in the toughest turns. The inside hand is at least as high as the outside hand, and reaching in the same direction.

The best skiers in the world strive for quiet, level arms. Those whose arm discipline is less than perfect usually admit that they would ski better if their arms did not move around so much. See figure 10.3 for an example of a skier demonstrating good arm discipline.

Try to keep your inside hand in your field of view at all times. If it is, it will at least be in the ball park. I myself ski better when I'm wearing white gloves, because they make me more aware of where my hands are.

Figure 10.3. Martina Ertl, winner of the 1998 World Cup giant slalom title and second overall, and one of the most technically sound skiers on the circuit. Her superb balance is aided by her well-disciplined arms. Her hands and shoulders are quiet and level at all times.

Avoid the common problem of reaching forward with your downhill hand to plant your pole. If you carry both of your arms up and in front of you at all times, little extra movement will be needed to plant your pole in the right place.

To help develop solid, quiet arms, try this: tie a five-foot piece of string into a loop. Put your hands in the loop, pull it tight, and go skiing. See figure 10.4. The loop helps put your hands where you want them, and will keep you from dropping one or the other. A few runs like this every now and then will improve your arm discipline and your lateral balance, significantly.

Linking Parallel Turns—The Challenge of Swapping Sides

Skiers pass a watershed when they learn to link parallel turns without widening their stance. This is, in my opinion, where advanced skiing starts.

Whenever you make a turn, your center of gravity must be closer to the center of the turn than the point at which the resultant meets the snow. See figure 10.5. And that point must be somewhere inside your base of support, or you will topple. As you start to turn in the other direction, the point moves to the other side of your center of gravity, still within your base of support.

If you are making gentle turns in a wedge or wide parallel stance, that point may stay well within the area enclosed by your skis without any extra movements on your part (figure 10.6). But as your stance gets narrower and centrifugal force gets bigger, the relationship between your center of gravity and feet must change significantly from turn to turn. To make linked, narrow-stance parallel turns, your center of gravity and feet must swap sides with every direction change (figure 10.7). That swap is called *crossover* by ski instructors, and doing it well is one of the keys to expert skiing.

PETE SONNTAG

Figure 10.4. Skiing with a loop of string around your hands is an excellent way to develop quiet, level arms.

Figure 10.5. Deborah Compagnoni. The skier must be inclined toward the center of every turn to balance against the lateral force from the snow. As a result, the feet must travel farther to the outside than the center of gravity, and a longer distance through each turn.

Falling Into the Turn

Inducing the center of gravity to move across the feet is a subtle skill that every skier must develop to progress from basic parallel skiing to the dynamic, fluid execution of expert arcs. To make that graceful transition from one turn to the next in a narrow stance requires you to estimate in advance how much centrifugal force you will feel once you have entered the upcoming turn and your skis have engaged the snow.

Figure 10.6. A wedge makes lateral balance easy: the resultant on the skier always stays within the base of support.

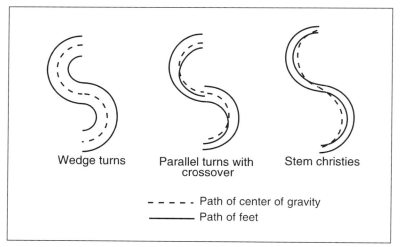

Wedge turns   Parallel turns with crossover   Stem christies

– – – – Path of center of gravity
———— Path of feet

Figure 10.7. The paths of the skier's center of gravity and feet in various types of turns.

You must, and this is the hardest part, let yourself *go out of balance and topple* from the old turn, across your skis and down the hill, toward the center of the new turn. How fast, and in exactly what direction you let yourself fall is dictated by a host of factors that only experience can teach you to recognize and evaluate.

This whole business is scary for skiers learning to make parallel turns. Being out of balance is something they have always worked hard to avoid. For skiers who have the judgment to know how much centrifugal force awaits them and when it will come, it is the source of one of skiing's great sensations: the weightless feeling of flying into the turn.

Learning to swap sides to link parallel turns, as shown in figure 10.8, is a bit like learning to walk. Both movements involve committing to a period of imbalance. A child makes his first unaided step by falling forward, then catching himself with an outstretched foot. That is how we all learned to walk. Eventually, the movements come smoothly and the moment of imbalance is invisible. Still, every step we make for the rest of our lives begins with a controlled fall.

To begin a parallel turn from a narrow stance, you must learn to make a controlled fall, too. The toddler falls forward anticipating the floor's support. You incline toward the center of the new turn, anticipating the lateral force from the snow that will support you later, once the ski has engaged the snow.

Going into a traverse between turns is like bringing your feet together and standing still between steps as you walk. Each turn and each step is separated by a period of static balance. Fluid movement starts when you move continuously and directly from one step to the next, and from one turn to the next.

In other words, skiing becomes much more interesting when you begin to add a transition phase to your turns. It is the watershed to advanced skiing. From here on, the transition becomes the focus of much of your attention.

Techniques for Swapping Sides

There are many good techniques for getting your center of gravity and feet to swap sides. An expert skier will use all the ones described here at one point or another in a day of skiing. A single turn will often incorporate dashes of several. Knowing them all, and mixing and matching them to the situation at hand, is a hallmark of good skiing.

Figure 10.8. To link parallel turns, both the skier's feet must swap sides with his center of gravity at the same time.

Stemming

The simplest way to accomplish the crossover between your feet and your center of gravity is to step the new outside ski outward into the new turn. This safely and securely establishes both a steering angle and the inward lean needed for the new turn. See figure 10.9.

After having learned to do this, many skiers spend the rest of their skiing careers trying not to. It is the stem turn initiation for which so many otherwise good skiers incessantly chastise themselves.

Some instructors contend that we should never learn to turn this way, that there are other ways to learn to ski that will never lead you to make a stem turn. It

Figure 10.9. By extending the uphill ski in a stem, the skier establishes both an initial steering angle and an inclined relationship between her center of gravity and new outside ski while she is supported by the downhill ski.

is as if the stem turn is a Venus flytrap technique that, once having been learned, will forever hold you in its clutches.

There is absolutely nothing wrong with learning to turn with an uphill stem. It is an essential and useful technique that the best skiers in the world use constantly, whether or not they recognize or admit it. The only reason skiers get stuck in it is that they do not learn other, more advanced techniques.

To get beyond the stem, you must first learn to link turns—it is much harder to start a parallel turn from a traverse than from the completion of another turn—and you must learn more advanced ways of getting your center of gravity and feet to swap sides.

Making Your Feet Slow Down

Any action that makes your feet slow down in relation to your upper body can be used to produce a crossover (figure 10.10). When you finish a turn against a mogul, for example, your feet slow down, the rest of your body keeps going, and they swap sides.

Other examples abound. A sharp edge set at the end of a turn will set the same mechanism in motion. Another case is the *preturn*, a maneuver that was commonly taught in ski schools in the 1950s and 1960s. In preparation for a turn from a traverse, the skier first made a small, sharp turn up the hill. His momentum would carry his body across his skis toward the center of the upcoming turn. Look closely at the skiers around you, and you will see this effect in many turns.

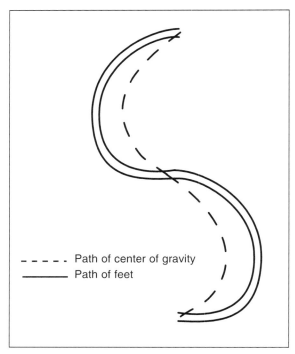

Figure 10.10. By making the feet turn more sharply at the end of the turn, you can get them to cross back under the path of your center of gravity.

Stepping to the Uphill Ski

Imagine you are in perfect balance on your downhill foot. What happens if you simply put your uphill foot on the snow and pick up your downhill foot? You fall down the hill.

This is an essential technique, seen most easily in medium to large turns, but also used in short turns. You stand on your uphill ski at the end of the turn, with the ski either on its uphill edge or flat on the snow, and lift your downhill ski (figures 10.11 and 10.12). As your center of gravity falls into the turn, you roll the new outside ski, the one to which you just stepped, onto its inside edge. As it changes edges, you twist it to the initial steering angle you need for the new turn.

Figure 10.11. In the second and third frames the skier lifts his downhill ski (check out its shadow) and begins to topple to his right, toward the center of the new turn. This establishes the inward lean he will need when the new outside ski engages the snow in the sixth frame.

Figure 10.12. Thomas Stangassinger steps to his uphill ski in the third frame, causing his body to topple toward his left and help establish the inclination he will need for the next turn.

Flexing

The techniques of passive and active flexion discussed in chapter 7, when performed in the completion phase of the turn, induce the path of the center of gravity to cross over that of the feet. Entering the completion phase of the turn, you quickly flex, either passively or actively. Now the snow is no longer pushing on your body. With no external force acting on you, your body no longer follows a curved path. Its momentum carries it in a straight line. Because your skis still have contact with the snow, however, they will continue to turn, carrying your feet with them. As a result, your body moves across your feet to start the new turn while your feet pass underneath, finishing the old one.

The feeling is of being released from the old turn. Your body flies across your feet into the new turn, and feels as if it is accelerating. The flexion must begin before the old turn in finished, giving you the feeling that your upper body is starting the new turn while your feet finish the old one (figure 10.13).

Active absorption is usually accompanied by a forward thrust of the feet. This combination of movements enhances the crossover, enabling you to make exceptionally dynamic transitions from one turn to the next. By bringing the feet forward, pressure is shifted back on the skis to where they are stiffer, thereby reducing their self-steering effect. This makes the skis go straighter, helping them hold. At the same time, the muscles that retract your legs also pull your torso forward and across the skis, accelerating the crossover. Once your feet have passed under your center of gravity, their continued forward thrust puts them well to the outside of the new turn, quickly setting up an aggressive inclination for the new turn.

As developments in ski equipment enable us to hold tighter and more aggressive turns, we need more inclination earlier in the turn. Such turns also produce larger virtual bumps, requiring greater ranges of extension and flexion. For these reasons, the importance of active flexion and extension have grown steadily through the years to the point where they are essential techniques for the best mogul skiers, racers, and experts carving turns.

Using Your Pole

When advanced skiers are faced with challenging situations, they often lose the confidence to commit their center of gravity into the turn ahead of their feet. They must still find a way to establish the inclination they need for the new turn, and

Figure 10.13. Andrej Miklavc of Slovenia uses active absorption and a step to the inside ski to cross over into the new turn.

usually adopt the safe alternative of an uphill stem. Quickly pivoting the skis and thrusting the tails to the side, usually with upper-body rotation, is an even worse alternative that we commonly see. This move quickly generates some lateral force against which to balance. Neither solution is a good one.

Once you have allowed your body's momentum to carry it across the skis and into the new turn, its motion can only be slowed at the beginning of the turn by a planted pole. Without a pole in the snow to hedge her bet, a skier will systematically underestimate how much commitment to make toward the new turn, because overcommitting can lead to a nasty fall down the hill. Undercommitting merely results in a poor turn.

The support of a properly planted pole allows you to commit fully to the turn without serious concern for overcommitting. If you let yourself go a bit too far toward the center of the new turn, the pole will be there for support. This requires that you plant the pole solidly, with a firm grip, and at the very beginning of the turn (figure 10.14).

Oftentimes when initiating a very short turn on a steep slope, an accomplished skier will quickly get his upper body across his feet and into the new turn, and suspend it there with his pole while he pivots his unweighted skis through the fall line.

Figure 10.14. In short turns on a steep slope, the pole plant is an essential support that enables the skier to commit to a strong crossover.

11

The View From Here

Our sport is going through some very exciting times. In recent years, equipment has advanced faster that it has since the late 1960s and early 1970s. Skis are so much easier to ski on, so much more versatile, and so much more fun than they were just a few years ago that everyone I know feels like a better skier. Snowmaking and grooming have become so sophisticated that even during poor snow years, the skiing is downright good. Even clothing has improved. New fabrics are so versatile that there is no longer any excuse for being too hot or too cold.

What has not changed, as corny as it sounds, is the feeling of the wind in your face and the snow under your feet; the freedom of moving expansively through

Figure 11.1.   Skiing well is its own lifelong reward.

space; the huge, insistent force of the mountain pulling you toward the valley; the intimate, emphatic engagement of your skis with the snow. These things are time-less. And even though we often feel as if we are discovering them for the first time, most of the movements we make to elicit these phenomena are as old as the sport.

My intent with this book has not been to present anything of my own inven-tion, but to illuminate with an expressive and hopefully clear light the techniques and methods that have been created by the collective genius of the world's best skiers. If, by doing so, I have helped increase your enjoyment of the sport, my time has been well spent.

Deborah Compagnoni.

Index

A

Aamodt, Kjetil Andre 44, 51, 96
airplane turns 3
alignment 50
Allais, Emile 97
Amiez, Sebastian 96, 122
angle of attack 21
angular momentum 13-14
angulation 105-112
    hip 108-112, 113-114
    knee 105-109, 110, 113-114
anticipation 90-92
arms 128
attack, angle of 21
Attacking Vikings 51
avalement 69

B

back flips 14
balance and balancing
    fore-aft 56, 59-60
    lateral 123-135
    on outside ski 125-128
    against snow's lateral force 123-124
binding lifters 115-122
Bjornsson, Kristinn 65, 66
blocking pole plant 93
boot canting 116-120
    lateral 116, 118
    overcanting 119
    undercanting 119
boot design
    forward lean 82-85
    special considerations for women 85
boot leverage 57

boots 27, 121-122
    heel lifts 86
    principal discriminants 81-82
boot stiffness 81-86
Braden, Vic vii
Bradley, Tami 54
braquage 89
bumps, virtual 37-38, 64-67
Buraas, Hans-Petter 18, 51

C

canting 116
    boot 116-120
    lateral 116, 118
    overcanting 119
    undercanting 119
carving 39-40
    key features of 40
    line selection for 44-46
center of gravity 9, 11-13
    in turns 130
coaching
    deep vii
    shallow vii
Colo, Zeno 93
comma position 101, 111
Compagnoni, Deborah 10, 34, 35, 36, 115, 129
compensating 15
countering
    coordinating with knee angulation 113-114
    exercises 112
    hip angulation and 110-112
counterrotation 101-102, 111
Coyote, Wile E. 73

critical edge angle 19-20, 26
crossover 128
     parallel turns with 130
custom footbeds 120-121

D

design
     boot 82-85
     ski 115-122
down. *See* up and down
downhill stem 28, 29
down-unweighting 73
     vs up-unweighting 73-74
Dynastar 36

E

edging 103-122
     modern 116
efficiency 63
Elan 115
equilibrium 15
Ertl, Martina 10, 89, 106, 108, 109, 127
exercises
     hip angulation and countering 112
     javelin turns 112, 113
     pivot slips 57, 59
     for quiet arms 128
external forces 5-6

F

Fédération Internationale de Ski (FIS) 115
feet
     slowing down 132
     in turns 130
Feynman, Richard 5
FIS. *See* Fédération Internationale de Ski
flex and flexing 133-134
     active 69-70
     longitudinal 23, 24-26
     passive 69-70
     torsional 23, 24
flips, back 14
footbeds 120-121
forces 5-8
     combining 12
     components of 13
     external 5-6
     on flying hand 21

internal 5
     reaction 7, 13, 124
     resultant 12
     from snow 6-7, 64, 70-76, 123-124
     twisting 13
     working with 11-13
fore and aft 53-62
     balance 56, 59-60
     moving 54-58
     pressure distribution factors 54
     synchronizing with turn phases 60-62
     uncoupling up and down from 76-78
     vs up and down 78
form and function 2-3
forward lean 82-85
     change effects 85
     on-the-hill augmentation 85
     testing 84
Fuerr, Art 112
full twists 14
Furuseth, Ole Christian 51

G

gender differences 111-112
     special considerations for women 85
Gerg, Hilde 10
German tidal wave 10
Girardelli, Marc 125
Grandi, Thomas 34
gravity, center of 9, 11-13
     in turns 130
grip on snow 18-20

H

hands 127-128
Hansson, Martin 90
Hart 112
heel lifts 86
heel-thrust 101
hip angulation 108-112
     coordinating with knee angulation 113-114
     and countering 110-112, 113-114
     exercises 112
     gender differences 111-112
hip rotation 99-101
     advantages of 100
     disadvantages of 101
     in powder snow 100
holding 103-104
Hrovat, Urska 115

I

ice 107
ice skates 103, 104
inertia 14
inside ski 17
internal forces 5

J

Jagge, Finn Christian 51, 96
javelin turns 112, 113
Joubert, Georges 69, 70, 89

K

Killy, Jean Claude 70
Kjellin, Sara 9
Kjus, Lasse 51
knee angulation 105-109
    hip angulation and countering with
        110, 113-114
Koznick, Kristina 41

L

lateral balance 123-135
lateral canting 116, 118
lateral force 123-124
learning 50-51
learning ratios 79-80
leg rotation 89-90, 91
leverage
    boot 57
    increased 115
linear momentum 13
linking parallel turns 128-130, 131
longitudinal flex 23, 24-26

M

Mahre, Phil 121
Mahre, Steve 121
Maier, Hermann 25
Mayer, Christian 45
mechanical principles 5-15
Miklavc, Andrej 134
Mittermier, Rosi 10
modern edging 116
Moe, Tommy 79

moguls 68
    common problems 68
    key technical ingredients 68
    up-unweighting 74
moment of inertia 14
momentum 8
    angular 13-14
    changes in 11
    linear 13
    working with 11-13
Moseley, Jonny 65
motion, skier's 17-29
motor learning 50-51
moving fore and aft 54-58
    basics 56
    synchronizing with turn phases 60-62
    vs up and down 78
moving up and down 63-86
    rationale for 63-67
    vs fore and aft 78

N

1998 Nagano Olympics 10
Neureuther, Christian 10
neutral point 57-58
Newton, Sir Isaac 5, 8
Newton's third law 101
Next Revolution 1-2
Norheim, Sondre 115
Nowen, Ylva 27, 62, 93

O

oblique pole plant 94
1998 Olympic Games 10
outside ski 17, 126
    balancing on 125-128
overcanting 119

P

parallel turns
    with crossover 130
    linking 128-130, 131
pivot slips 57, 59
pole(s), using 134-135
pole plants 93, 95, 96, 135
    blocking 93
    oblique 94
    torque from 93-95

pole vault effect 75
powder skiing 98
    hip rotation in 100
pressure 7-8
pressure fore and aft
    controlling 55
    distribution factors 54
preturn 132

R

ratios 79-80
reaction force 7, 13, 124
rebound 75-76
redirecting skis 87
resultant forces 12
reverse camber 24
reverse-shoulder 101, 111
rewards 137
Riegler, Claudia 108, 109, 122
Ronnback, Jesper 81, 83
Rossignol Strato 115
rotation
    counterrotation 101-102
    hip 99-101, 100, 101
    leg 89-90, 91
    upper-body 97-98, 100, 101
rubber band effect 75
Russel, Patrick 125

S

Schifferer, Andreas 125
Schleper, Sarah 117
Schneider, Hannes 97
Seizinger, Katja 10, 35, 48, 73
self-steering effect 23-26
    controlling 28
shallow coaching vii
sidecut 23-24
    curved 26
sides, swapping 128-130
    techniques for 131-135
ski(s) 17-29
    boot as part of 27
    controlling interaction with snow 47-51
    design effects 115-122
    edging 103-122
    fore and aft 53-62
    grip on snow 18-20
    holding 103-104

for ice 107
initial steering angle 42-46
inside 17
neutral point 57-58
outside 17, 125-128
for powder skiing 98
redirecting 87
turning 87-102
uphill 132, 133
slowing 11, 20-21
slowing down your feet 132
snow 17-29
    controlling interaction with 47-51
    forces from 6-7, 13, 70-76
    lateral force from 123-124
    penetrating 18-19
    perfect force from 64
    powder 98, 100
    reaction force from 7, 13, 124
    reducing force from 70-76
snow-up skiing 1-3
Stangassinger, Thomas 95, 96, 133
steeps 126
steering angles 22, 23, 24
    initial 42-46
    size of 43-44
stem christies 130
stemming 131-132
Stenmark, Ingemar 51, 58, 117
stepping to uphill ski 132, 133
Stiansen, Tom 51
stiffness, boot 81-86
swapping sides 128-130
    techniques for 131-135
swing weight 14
Sykora, Thomas 61, 87, 96

T

technique 47-51
    for swapping sides 131-135
Telemark stance 60, 61
terrain unweighting 74-75
Thoeni, Gustavo 58, 117
Tomba, Alberto 57, 58, 93, 96, 117
toppling 15
torques 13
    from pole plant 93-95
torsional flex 23, 24
trail maps 84, 85, 120
Trinkl, Hannes 33

turns and turning 11, 20-21
  airplane 3
  anatomy of 31-46
  anticipation 90-92
  back flips 14
  carved 39-40, 44-46
  checked 42
  completion 33-34
  control 33, 34
  counterrotation 101-102
  falling into 129-130
  feet 89
  full twists 14
  hip rotation 99-101, 100, 101
  initiation 32
  javelin turns 112, 113
  leg rotation 89-90, 91
  linking 128-130, 131
  options 28, 29
  parallel 128-130, 131
  path of skier's center of gravity and feet
    in 130
  phases of 31-34
  preturn 132
  rebound 76
  self-steering effect 23-26
  skidded 40-41
  skis 87-102
  steeps 126
  synchronizing with fore-aft movements
    60-62
  taxonomy of 38-42
  Telemark 60, 61
  transition 33, 34, 35
  twisters 102
  types of 38-39, 130
  upper-body rotation 97-98, 100, 101
  wedge 130
twisters 102
twisting actions 13-14
twists, full 14

U

undercanting 119
unweighting 70-76
  down-unweighting 73-74
  rebound 75-76
  terrain 74-75
  up-unweighting 72, 73-74
up and down 63-86
  meaning of 67

rationale for 63-67
uncoupling from fore and aft 76-78
vs fore and aft 78
uphill ski, stepping to 132, 133
upper-body rotation
  advantages of 100
  disadvantages of 101
  mechanics of 99
up-unweighting 72
  with moguls 74
  rebound 75-76
  vs down-unweighting 73-74

V

vertical. *See* up and down
virtual bumps 37-38
  accounting for 64-67
Vogelreiter, Siegfried 27, 96
Von Gruenigen, Michael 96
Vuarnet, Jean 89

W

Wassmier, Markus 10
wedeln 101
wedge turns 130
weighting 70
  swing weight 14
  unweighting 70-76
Weinbrecht, Donna 69, 91
windup/release 90
women 111-112
  special considerations for 85
World Cup 10, 14, 25

Z

Zurbriggen, Primin 25, 121-122

About the Author

TIM HANCOCK

Ron LeMaster has spent more than 25 years as a ski instructor and race coach. Currently an instructor, trainer, and lecturer at the Vail/Beaver Creek Ski School, he has also taught at the Aspen Ski School and coached with the Aspen Ski Club and the University of Colorado.

Certified and accredited by the Professional Ski Instructors of America, LeMaster has spent much of the past six years lecturing at ski schools in the Colorado Rockies on the topic of ski technique and biomechanics. A frequent contributor to skiing magazines, he has also written technical literature for the Professional Ski Instructors of America. He holds degrees in mechanical engineering and computer science. LeMaster lives in Boulder, Colorado, where he enjoys skiing, kayaking, and cycling.

Color enlargements of many of the photomontages appearing in this book are available from the author. For more information, write to:

Front Range Images
4462 Wellington Road
Boulder, CO 80301

MORE BOOKS for SKIERS

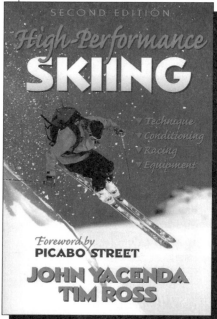

High-Performance Skiing combines the latest in expert instruction, technique, and conditioning with breakthroughs in equipment technology to help you negotiate the most difficult runs. This book offers an up-front, how-to approach for revving up your skiing and racing, along with timely tips on how to handle a variety of skiing situations.

This instructive guide further explores high-performance techniques and skills that will lead to more consistent performance, greater versatility, less fatigue, greater endurance, increased strength and flexibility, and more confidence.

Item PYAC0713 • ISBN 0-88011-713-3 • $17.95 ($26.95 Canadian)

If you've been wondering how to get started in the exciting sport of backcountry skiing or if you're looking to brush up on your backcountry skills, this book has all the information you need.

Author Jean Vives shares the wisdom gained from his 30-plus years of backcountry skiing experience as he presents the essential tools of the trade, from the exercises to get you in peak shape to the best clothing and equipment to use. Stay safe and on-course with detailed descriptions of winter camping, navigation, mountain weather, avalanche detection, and survival techniques. Put this book in your pack and find out how much fun backcountry skiing can be.

Item PVIV0650 • ISBN 0-88011-650-1 • $18.95 ($27.95 Canadian)

HUMAN KINETICS
The Premier Publisher for Sports & Fitness
P.O. Box 5076, Champaign, IL 61825-5076
www.humankinetics.com

2335

To place your order, U.S. customers call **TOLL FREE 1-800-747-4457.**
Customers outside the U.S. place your order using the appropriate
telephone number/address shown in the front of this book.

Join the growing number of people who are discovering the fun and fitness benefits of snowshoeing! Edwards and McKenzie, avid snowshoers and cofounders of a sport snowshoe manufacturing company, make it easy for you to learn the basics. They discuss choosing the proper equipment, snowshoeing techniques, guidelines for safety, and a training plan to get your body in shape for this sport.

The book also provides descriptions of 45 of the world's best snowshoeing destinations and information on additional activities that complement snowshoeing.

Item PEDW0767 • ISBN 0-87322-767-0 • $13.95 ($19.50 Canadian)

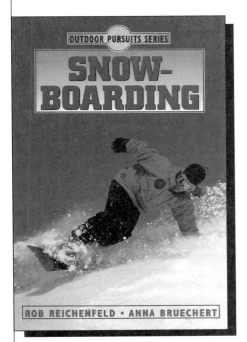

Snowboarding helps beginners get started and veterans get better! Less-experienced riders will discover tips for waxing and storing boards and sharpening their edges, along with advice for falling safely and riding through soft snow. More advanced participants will learn how to get started in freestyle, racing, and riding on ungroomed trails. And everyone will appreciate the hints on handling crowds and finding the best snow.

This book also includes advice on selecting the right board and accessories, in-depth explanations of key snowboarding skills, and detailed descriptions of 20 of the world's best snowboarding resorts—from authors who have been there.

Item PREI0677 • ISBN 0-87322-677-1 • $13.95 ($19.50 Canadian)

Cross-Training for Sports is the first book to provide expert guidance on how to add new forms of training to your workouts, how much training to add, and when to add it. The best strength exercises and stretches for 26 different sports, including Alpine skiing, are illustrated and fully explained, taking the guesswork out of setting up a program.

Coaches and athletes will be able to develop personalized training programs to target areas for improvement and choose from the best sports and activities to improve aerobic endurance. The authors fully explain the training principles involved in cross-training, and they provide a detailed breakdown of the aerobic and anaerobic needs for each sport.

Item PMOR0493 • ISBN 0-88011-493-2 • $19.95 ($29.95 Canadian)